For R.M.W.
from A.C.B.
May. 1978

Precarious Living

Precarious Living

The Path to Life

by

MARTIN ISRAEL

HODDER AND STOUGHTON
LONDON SYDNEY AUCKLAND TORONTO

My thanks are due to Denis Duncan for his invaluable help
in the arrangement of this book.

From the unreal lead me to the real, from darkness lead
me to light, from death lead me to immortality.

(BRIHADARANYAKA UPANISHAD, 1:3:28)

We know that we have passed from death unto life,
because we love the brethren

(1 JOHN 3:14).

Contents

A Vision

I WAS PROCEEDING downwards into the darkness by a constantly descending spiral staircase. Around me was a vast army of nameless people with faceless countenances and inarticulate voices. All the world was there in noiseless tumult, and yet I was completely alone. At the bottom of the staircase was a plateau crowded with people who were mere shadows and wraiths. In the centre was the pit.

The pit enveloped all who descended into it in a final darkness. We were all progressing towards it.

I was accompanying this funereal procession, orderly in its disorder, separate from it and yet integral with it. I too had to descend to the deepest depth, and yet I did not know why this had to be. Feelings of fear and resentment began to well up in me, for I did not want to leave the world thus.

Suddenly a wisp of air blew at me from a nameless face. It said; "I am the way, I am the truth and I am life; no one comes to the Father except by me."

I went my way in peace with thanksgiving.

Prologue

OUR LIFE ON earth is an invitation to partake fully of the glory of the world. This glory consists, certainly, of the material riches of the earth, but there is something more in store for us. It is the discovery of the core of identity deep within us that survives the changes of the world outside us, and grows in stature, even when the material world falls from us at the moment of death. We are not fully alive until we can confirm, through the experience of our life, that inner core which is our proof of purpose, meaning, and destiny.

How this identity may be recognised and how we may grow into full persons is the theme of this book. It is also the meaning of the spiritual life.

I have started, deliberately, with a personal testimony. The reader must surely demand an autobiographical sketch from one who dares to outline the path of authentic existence. I have then tried to define some words and concepts that are important in understanding the spiritual life. Finally I have described various paths towards enlightenment, and the hazards that may follow an unwise devotion to any one system of belief or to techniques of self-development that ignore our duty to our fellow creatures.

Every experience in life is a key to deeper understanding provided we have the wisdom to be still and ask the right questions. Wisdom comes, not primarily through external authorities, but from the depths within us that experience life's vicissitudes. This wisdom can then be augmented by the great store of human understanding that has been collected in the world's sacred scriptures over the ages. We can, in turn, give of our own store to the world for the sake of those who follow after us.

This is the way to authentic life.

I
One Man's Path

1

The Call

THERE IS A call in the silence that leads man to the fulfilment of his life. It leads one on from the trivial round of surface living in the company of those who are travelling along a well-worn way that returns to its point of departure, and reveals a more solitary uphill path away from the crowd. It is there that the inner voice of meaning declares itself. The voice may, of course, be disregarded. It is always disturbing those who would prefer to avoid a life of deeper significance. But to those who are responsive, there is an abandonment of the world of ever-changing passions and fantasies and an entry into that timelessness of abiding reality which interpenetrates the world of form and gives it meaning.

To some the call comes at the depth of distress or disillusionment, when, through the debris of a shattered relationship or a frustrated ambition, a glimpse of a way of living more perfect than mere self-gratification is afforded. This is not to be dismissed as wishful thinking, for the impulse comes spontaneously. Like a flash of lightning, it illuminates the personality and the world around it. It inspires hope into the dejected heart, and lightens the way forward with faith. Out of the ashes of past disappointments, a new life emerges like a phoenix. To others the call is a stirring within that follows the witnessing of a deed of great self-sacrifice, or the inspiration of eloquent words, or a noble work of art. The action or the perfection of the art is an outer testimony to the eternity of life that is so often hidden beneath the blind meaninglessness of selfish living. The spontaneous kindness that may flow from even the most unlikely people during a period of emergency may effect a change in awareness in those who observe it. A full participation in the glory of nature may lift the consciousness of the person beyond himself to an identification with the greater community of creation.

Sometimes the call has strongly religious overtones. It may come from the lips of a preacher, or the pages of scripture, or the liturgy during an act of worship. What may before have passed unnoticed, now suddenly speaks to the person's deepest need. Indeed, it is difficult to gain a real understanding of the Bible until one's own experiences in life have confirmed and illuminated its deepest teaching. Whatever the means of awakening, the voice speaks from the depths of one's personality and leads one, by a new and living way, to the life of eternity. The voice is the light that emanates from the deepest part of the personality, the most real point in the identity of any person, the part that is called the true self, or the soul.

In my life the call came very early. I was not more than three years old when I heard, with the inward ear, a voice that addressed me directly in the darkness of my inner self, yet carried with it a radiant light. It gave me a preview of the pattern of my life, and showed me the path I had to follow to be an authentic person. The path was a fearsome one. I was to pass along a dark and ever-narrowing tunnel, alone and isolated, and to move further and further away from all personal contact towards a dark, undisclosed future. There was to be no outer comfort. I was to be shriven of all the reassurances that come from everyday human contact in my journey along that solitary road. I would be lonely and often misunderstood, yet I would be driven onwards by the power of real life. I would never know that superficial peace that comes with a narrow outer conformity to my surroundings. I would be compelled to go on in order to find and fulfil the real work in my life, even to its culmination in the darkness of death. Yet even at this age, I had an intimation that death was not the end, that the humiliation and suffering of a life lived in honesty were the necessary precursors of glorification. That glorification would no longer be entirely personal. It embraced all people.

I can forgive the reader's incredulous amazement at this account of a small child's vision of his future life. Its precocity is so staggering that I can excuse the sceptic's conclusion that its author has interposed adult insights into a child's mind. But this is not so. The vision of reality that showed me my life's work did not infuse me with self-esteem or happiness. I had a terrible sense of dereliction. I howled at the intimation of darkness, lack of comprehension, and loneliness. The burden was almost too great to bear, and yet I knew that I had to persist in faith and never betray the knowledge that had been given me.

The call leads one away from the mass of humanity, at least in the earliest stages. There is a constant awareness of the danger of contamination by the mindless thinking that is the preserve of many people. It is easy to slip back into the selfish life of those around one, and to betray the great vision. This period of withdrawal is a necessary stage in the spiritual life, and, if one is fortunate, one meets a friend who can guide one on the lonely uncharted way. In due course one has to re-join the human company, but not before one has acquired the inner strength to retain one's integrity in the face of all outer distractions.

When the way is shown early in one's life, this period of withdrawal is fraught with additional hardships, which if courageously confronted, lead to an enormous strengthening of personality. It is a law of life that the more one gives of one's life in faith, the more fully does one grow into a knowledge of life. Faith is both the way towards fulfilment of one's destiny and the meaning of that destiny. For it does not arise from within, but is rather infused into one as a gift by the Spirit of God.

I realised very soon that my parents, admirable people that they were in many respects, were not those to whom I could confide my deepest thoughts. Such excursions from the well-worn world of daily events would have embarrassed and alarmed them, living, as we did, in affluent South Africa during the inter-war period. As an only child I had few of my own age with whom to talk, so I was thrown back on the company of the African servants employed in my home. It was through these servants that I was able to pass along the testing ground of inner authenticity. Their companionship was the light that led me on towards the early fulfilment of what I had been shown. They were simple, unlettered folk, but the unerring inner vision of a child saw in them an authenticity of character completely lacking in the Europeans I knew. In these humble servants, in their silence as well as in their joyful song, I sensed spiritual reality. The characteristics of spirituality are almost impossibly difficult to define, yet they are so wholly obvious to a child's discernment. Perhaps the most immediate quality of the spiritual person is his outflowing nature, a nature which allows of direct communication both on a physical and a psychical level. In other words, one is at once aware of the deep bond that binds one to another, a bond that does not depend on sharing mutually held opinions, but is one which emanates from the core of personality and reaches the other persoon in the deepest concern. Such concern may certainly develop in the personality of many lesser people after a lifetime's association with someone else; they are in fact growing gradually into the experience of love, which is the crowning glory of the spiritual life as well as its foundation. But those who have already attained some measure of spiritual maturity can effect a deep relationship with many different types of people. They regard their fellow men not as objects to be used, but as souls to be cherished through the experience of identification with them.

The test of such a relationship is the ease of contact and the silence of the communication. In the silence truth speaks; it requires no guile or conviviality, but is completely free. These servants, who had little of their own in terms of worldly possessions, were unencumbered with pride, resentment, or covetousness. They could live in the present, which is also the realm of eternity. Alas, their kind has unfortunately disappeared. Their successors have assimilated much that is worst in modern European civilisation — its concern for immediate gratification of the senses, its contempt for values, and its

disbelief in an abiding order of righteousness — yet the
African soul still radiates through this superficial dross. I know
that, as a child, I felt most fully myself when I could be as one
of them.

It was through a servant girl that I came to understand the
source of the vision that had led me along the path of solitude.
Barely literate herself, she showed me a simple evangelical
tract that she had been given. It spoke of a man who had loved
the world sufficiently to take on its full burden of sin, and who
had died a terrible death for the world's redemption. I did not
come of a family that accepted this view of salvation, but the
knowledge of this man pierced me to the marrow of my being.
I knew in my depths that it was he who had spoken to me, and
that, however much I might disagree with what was said about
him, I could never turn away from his life and his solemn
witness to the truth.

My work was to be one of reconciliation.

2

The Light on the Path

THE PATH TOWARDS an authentic life is also the path towards a knowledge of God. In travelling along this path one appears to live in two worlds, a world of spiritual reality in which the highest values are the measure of ultimate meaning, and an earthly world in which survival and satisfaction of the body are the most pressing concerns. One soon learns that the two have to be actively confronted and properly integrated: a life that neglects material needs cannot attain spiritual reality, whereas material concern devoid of spiritual awareness ends in frustration and failure.

In my own early life the impression of spiritual reality was stamped indelibly in the deep centre of my personality, that is the soul, or spiritual self. The secret lay hidden within, but I had also to act in a way becoming to a child, which meant assuming a respectful attitude to teachers, many of whom I knew were devoid of deeper understanding, and being congenial to my fellows, who were more concerned about games and physical exercise than the life of the spirit. In the beginning of the spiritual ascent it is all too easy to become other-worldly and to lose concern for humanity. Two baneful results accrue from this: a general impotence in asserting oneself in the world, so that one is bullied and overridden, and a reciprocal feeling of contempt for those who behave insensitively to one. At the same time there is a deep, incoherent awareness of black evil around one, an evil that shows itself as an anonymous external power seeking to destroy the vision of completeness vouchsafed one, and leading one into a negative state of selfish living that culminates in a loss of identity within a dark shapeless mass of lifeless debris that was once living men. It follows that the two dangers lurking at the beginning of the path of life are a fear of occult attack by those who reject the vision of the aspirant, and exclusiveness, which is an unconscious reaction to the insecurity experienced within. At any age these fearsome adversaries can lead to a state of isolation not far removed from despair. When a child has to cope with them, they either break him completely or else they are surmounted. When the latter is achieved, the child begins to understand the meaning of authenticity and the exercise of free will.

My ineptitude in purely physical endeavours, such as games and creative manual work, not only made me an easy victim for bullying by those stronger than I, but also left me with a disconcerting sense of unreality in my relationships with other children. How different these superficial encounters were when compared with the silent communion I had with the African servants. To defend myself in the face of a hostile, uncomprehending crowd, I developed the mental side of my character. It must always have been powerful, as witnessed by my immediate grasp of the significance of the vision I had been given when only very young. But until my school days it lay dormant. Instead I was in direct communion with people and nature, and lived in harmony with my surroundings. It was through intellectual mastery that I held my own in an alien environment, and earned respect from those who would otherwise have unwittingly crushed me.

I must have been a strange child! Silence I loved more than anything else. In it I was in perpetual communion with my surroundings and with a world far greater than my physical surroundings. Each object, each flower, the sky and the atmosphere were bathed in a supersensual radiance. Each created thing pulsated with a life that was far more intimate than the coarse, movable life of worldly activity. In the darkness of night there was an even brighter light, the light of tumultuous silence in which the story of creation was celebrated in everlasting glory. Each object, no matter how little, was supreme, for God had made it and it reflected, in its own humility, the divine imprint. Each human face was pulsating with hidden meaning. That there was so much dull incomprehension of the very vision of life eternal was overwhelming in its sadness for me. In the depths of receptive silence no secret remains hidden. One's own inner life becomes open and transparent.

But the world does not know of this mystical reality that sustains the life of flux in which we all have to graduate to a measure of full personality. People lose sight of the embracing love that bears up all creation in its everlasting arms when they are immersed in surface living from day to day. How could I be understood — especially when I lived in a twilight zone between mystical light that was uncreated and the darkness of material and psychical evil? This evil was not related especially to my home, which was a place of beauty and warmth, but to the whole created universe which had been corrupted and desecrated by the selfish actions of its creatures, especially the angelic hierarchy and men, since the time of willed disobedience to the law of life, which is love for all things and for God who created them. No one who lives in full awareness, and has not blinded himself to reality by the abuse of intellectual ratiocination, can fail to feel the full power of psychic darkness which has been personified in various religious traditions as the devil. And some of this darkness has been assimilated by personalities, even our own, when they have been in a negative, destructive frame of mind. The end of evil is the complete destruction of the person, yet that word should mean the unique identity of every creature and especially of man, in whom personality is developed to its supreme degree, at least in the experience of the world we inhabit. This destruction is both an incorporation into nothingness and an annihilation of all uniqueness. It is the final result of living in isolation oblivious of the full body of mankind, and is an ever-present menace lurking for any whose life is selfish and centred in ignorance. The words of the Compline exhortation always ring audibly in my inward ear: "Be sober, be vigilant; because your adversary the devil, as a roaring lion, walketh about, seeking whom he may devour: whom resist steadfast in the faith" (I Peter 5:8). One learns in the course of life that evil has no primary, or substantive existence, but is the psychic residue left after a selfish, unredeemed action. What it is important to realise is that evil can never simply be averted. It *must* be confronted in the power of love and redeemed by love. I know now, as I glimpsed then as a child, that He who came to me could alone redeem evil, for He was love.

In the sombre progress through fear, ineptitude, and foreboding the light of reality breaks forth at every moment of full consciousness. Though the path of inner dereliction was already charted, I could escape from its overpowering pressure by an act of full participation in life. Joy comes from within; it is assuredly present in the world, but it does not come to us merely from agreeable outer circumstances. Rather it is the radiant joy from within ourselves, the knowledge of God immanent in our own being, that sheds radiance on the world, raising it from the corruption of mortality to the splendour of eternity. Joy came to me whenever I could centre my attention, in childlike wonder, on any phenomenon or object. As I have said, I knew, early in my life, the joy of identification with nature in her many forms: the countryside with its changing pattern of beauty, from spring blossoms to the yellow summer grassland, the flowers of the field, the autumn tints of brown and red, and the sharp cleansing winter barrenness when all was desolate and yet full of that true beauty that comes of a shriven landscape. In nature there is not merely the outer form, but also an inner realm that palpitates with psychic and spiritual life. To him who can observe there is nothing empty save the emptiness of a vapid, selfish human being intent only on himself and his needs.

I also knew the joy that comes from intellectual contemplation. When a mathematical problem is solved, and its solution sheds light on the fundamental properties of form, there is a momentary release of tension, and the mysterious glory of the universe is comprehended. The scientist studying the innermost secrets of life and the substance of life in its many manifestations can, in a moment of self-abandon, see clearly into the mind of Him who is the source of creation. This awareness came to me somewhat later in life, but I had an understanding of the supreme joy that follows pure mental activity when I was still a child, and this helped to sustain me in my lonely path.

What was painfully lacking in my life was human contact with my peers. This lack was accentuated by a paralysing shyness and social ineptitude. It is clear to me now that I was not properly earthed as a child; the spirit, as it were, had not fully incarnated. I could roam with facility in realms of mental speculation, but I doubted the efficacy of my own bodily actions.

This observation seems to me to be of theoretical importance in assessing the nature of the mystical temperament. The true mystic is born and not made. He is not really of this world at all, so, if his life is to be successful, he has to learn to come down to earth and mix fully with all sorts and conditions of men. His task is the reverse of that of the much more common earth-bound man, who, if he is to succeed fully, has to move beyond personal acquisitiveness to universal sympathy. How fortunate it is that both types of people inhabit the world, for one is essential to the other while neither is to be regarded as superior to the other.

My first real contact with people as individuals came significantly once again through African servants. I can remember an enormously fat African woman who used to do the family washing each Monday morning. She washed the linen in a large tub with a scrubbing board out in the open yard. One Monday she failed to arrive. When I enquired about her I was told quite perfunctorily that she had died of pneumonia during the week. This news pierced me, for though I had hardly ever spoken to her, I felt I knew her, and the circumstances of her death seemed unjust to me. This awareness of the monstrous injustice visited upon the African population became ever more strong. When I was eight years old I met the boy-friend of a servant maid. He was a coloured man, extremely intelligent and with a genius for mechanical things, but because of his colour he could get no work equal to his abilities. He was also a heavy drinker. One night he came in with flesh wounds following a drunken fracas. I was fascinated with the contrast of colour between his brown skin and the pink flesh of his chest wall! It was the first intimation I had of my future medical career, though my father was himself an eye-specialist. Even more important to me, however, were the circumstances that had led to this assault. How wrong it was that a person of such manifest intelligence should have to spend his life so wastefully! Shortly afterwards he was killed in a fight. The seeds of social awareness had been well implanted in my consciousness by these and other similar experiences. Indeed, I was an ardent socialist by the age of eight, though later experiences caused me to modify my political views without in any way decreasing my identification with the downtrodden and the abused.

Another early revelation was the evil of capital punishment, which was carried out quite often where I lived, usually on Africans. While I did not condone the violence of murder or rape, I realised that it was often the community that was as much to blame as the criminal, and that many self-satisfied, respectable, outwardly religious white people who exploited the Africans shamelessly were as eligible for the gallows as were the criminals themselves. Much of this moral insight was to be confirmed later when I was shown aspects of the after-life. Evil can never be expelled, not even in the life beyond death. It has to be faced directly with love. Only thus can it be redeemed. It is easier far to start this long process of redemption here on earth than in the indeterminate mental realms of the after-life. Moreover, the damage caused by resentment is much less severe while it is earthed than when it flows unimpeded in a psychic environment.

What I lacked in the way of outer companionship, I gained from reading the world's great classics. Indeed, it was the masterpieces of literature that were my inspiration rather than the classics of religious or mystical thought — apart from the Bible. I have always been grateful for this. Had I come of a family that indulged in mystical speculation or psychical research, I would quite naturally have assimilated the current trend of thought and repeated it automatically. The fact that the mystical sense was inborn in me and not cultivated by my background made it much more authentic. I started to read books on these subjects many years later, and, though I found

much that encouraged me and confirmed what had already
been revealed to me, I can honestly say that I never learned
anything from them that was new to me. From this one can
induce that the knowledge of spiritual things is given through
one's experience of life, which means living in receptive
awareness of the contrary influences around one. It can never
be acquired second-hand from the writings or words of other
people. Such instruction, if assimilated at all, remains merely a
mental edifice. When the rains descend, the floods rise, and the
winds blow and beat upon the house of intellectual knowledge,
it falls down. Only the house built upon the rock of faith
founded on spiritual experience can withstand the onslaught of
the elements, as Jesus taught His disciples at the end of the
Sermon on the Mount. It is this paucity of real spiritual
knowledge that lies at the root of the failure of conventional
religion to satisfy the inner hunger of modern man.

As I grew into early adolescence, so the glory of the world's
great thought and music filled my heart, inspiring me to fulfil
the vision that had come to me so long before. But each day
brought nearer the foreboding of utter loneliness, the time
when I would be completely uprooted, and left with nothing
but memories of the past. I knew that this period of aesthetic
and intellectual fulfilment was merely an interlude, a time of
recreation, before the real test began. I was living in a mental
world, delectable and ethereal, but with no direct participation
in the world of form. I can see now that this phase, far from
being a period of reprehensible self-indulgence at the expense
of others, was a vital preparation for what I had to do later on.
The Holy Spirit works best through a well-trained, healthy
mind. It is as much a duty to imbibe the beauties of life as to
work in the shadow regions amongst the derelict, for without
the knowledge of that beauty and its promise of universal
redemption, there would be no message to give the derelict and
broken-hearted. But my heart was broken too, even in the
heights of mental stimulation and aesthetic delight, for I was in
psychic contact with those who suffered, especially in the
German concentration camps during the period of the Nazi
regime. Though I was thousands of miles away and therefore

physically safe, an awareness of the overpowering evil that filled the world obsessed me. Through the gift of precognition, I found all too often that my worst fears were later confirmed. And yet even in this awareness of darkness and sin, there was the vital realisation that all men are members one of another, and no one who is a full person can isolate himself from injustice anywhere in the world.

It is the way he deals with this injustice that marks out the spiritual man from the superficial rabble-rouser who uses social injustice only to further his own ends.

3

Illumination

THE MYSTICAL LIFE is divided classically into the stages of purgation, illumination, and union. This is in fact a very simplified account of the soul's progress to the full encounter with God. Purgation ends only when eternal union has been attained; in this world there was one alone who attained this union fully, the Incarnate Christ. Illumination is to be seen not merely as a single blinding experience of God's radiance, but rather as a repeated awareness of God's love during the taxing round of purgation which leads the mystic on to the final unitive experience.

Such minor illuminations have been very much a part of my own life. They came to me even as a small child, and made me aware early of the redemptive value of suffering. It was particularly when I had been brought low through some outer circumstance, nearly always following a minor fall from grace, that I was most aware of God's love, and could progress once more in greater assurance of divine presence. There does, however, come in the lives of many aspirants an illumination of very much greater magnitude than this. Such an experience is a landmark, and it forms the foundation of further understanding and aspiration. Such an illumination came to me in early adolescence.

Up to that time, I was becoming more and more obsessed with the idea of finitude. I could glimpse in my mind's eye the end of all space, for it seemed to me that the whole universe was finite, that there was a definite end to it. Was there anything outside the universe, or was the universe the total reality? If I envisaged the latter possibility, I would have a sensation of intolerable enclosedness, a "cosmic claustrophobia". But if there was more to reality than merely the form of the universe, what was its nature and meaning? To be sure there was no person who could enlighten me, and the type of religious thought, superficial as it was, that I encountered could not envisage God in other than limited personal terms. Already I had experienced an ecstatic state when I contemplated the excellence and completeness of geometry. Even simple forms, like the triangle and the circle, had enclosed within them immutable laws of nature. I saw God in the very excellence of the form, and in the point of intersection of concurrent lines within the form.

When I was sixteen years of age, I was preparing for the final matriculation examination at the end of the year. I was considered an outstanding pupil, and I usually came first in the class. This was due, not so much to my mental abilities as to my obsessional attention to detail. Furthermore, my very security on earth depended on my excellent examination results, for my vulnerability was so extreme that a "bad" result, such as coming third or fourth in the class, would have been a major disaster. In a preparatory examination written some four months before the final test, I had done rather disappointingly in a mathematics paper. I had passed, but not very well. I returned home that day in a rather dispirited state of mind, and after supper repaired to bed. There I listened to my radio.

The overture to Weber's opera "Oberon" was announced, and I listened in pleasant anticipation, for although it was not a special favourite of mine I knew and liked the music very much. After a minute or so I suddenly became aware of an alteration in my perception. The music became blurred and indistinct, and at the same time the bedroom was bathed in a light of iridescent radiance so that its outlines and furniture could no longer be delineated. I was filled with a menacing fear that lasted for a mere instant, but then, as soon as I submitted to the experience, the fear disappeared and its place was taken by a sense of uplift and peace that I had never previously known.

I knew that the essential part of myself, the true self or soul, was raised far above the physical body, which I could no longer see or sense; for all physical sensation had been obliterated by a new type of sensory knowledge that came not from any bodily organs, but from the soul itself. I was borne aloft by a power that surpassed my understanding. It had no limitation but was all-pervading. Its thrust was irresistible and its action benefi-cent. It was the full measure of love, for with it were all things, and in it life found its consummation. Though formless and beyond description, it showed itself in a harmony of silence which was the very origin of all vibration and music. It was indeed a celestial music, not of sequence but of eternity. The dark stillness of this eternal power was also the incomparable radiance of light, a light so intense that it illuminated the source of life and cast its heavenly rays on the meaning and communion of life. The uncreated light was the primary energy of the power of eternity, and the heavenly music of eloquent silence was its emanation into the soul.

I was no longer in the universe at all, but in the realm of eternal life which is neither past nor future but only the ever-living present. I had been lifted to a height above all measurable heights. I was able, in this situation, to perceive the entire created world, for I was outside it. I "saw" and "heard" with the "eyes" and "ears" of the soul which also "felt" the loving impact of the supreme power that embraced and raised me. In the language of science the nearest description would be one of sensing with an inner, hidden organ of perception that included all five senses, each and all functioning in a magni-fied, transformed awareness. Furthermore, the information obtained was integrated by an inner organ of intelligence into a coherent system of supersensual purpose and meaning.

In my situation beyond creation I could divine the onward flow of life in the cosmos. I was aware of the perpetual cycle of life: countless generations of creatures lived, suffered, died, and were reborn. This cycle continued until the creature attained fullness of being. It was not simply an unending round of life, death, and rebirth, but rather one that had, as its end, the perfect union of creature with Creator. This ascending spiral of life, death, and rebirth was seen to be the destiny of all living things in their progress towards completion. The struggle and termination of each life were comparable, in relation to divine reality, to the tearful resistance of little children who are put to bed by their parents, and who awake fresh the next day to advance on new adventures. I was filled with an irresistible sense of humour and delight when I realised that the pain borne by the creature was trivial in comparison with the glory that was to be revealed in him and in the whole world at the end of the human struggle. The entire created universe was shown to me symbolically as a gigantic sphere whose movement was discernible as a minute turn of a wheel, but this movement encompassed countless generations of human beings over a vast time-scale.

As these spiritual truths were being revealed to me, I suddenly was aware that my own personality had been transformed. I was no longer a separate, isolated unit. Although I had not lost my identity — indeed, for the first time in my life I had really experienced the identity of a whole person — I was in union with all creation and my identity was added to it, giving of its essence to the created whole. In this state of expanded consciousness, I had transcended private existence. But at the moment of bliss, when union was realised, I felt myself being gradually, but decisively lowered. As this occurred, my personality became dominant once more and rebelled against this descent from the realm of eternal life. Indeed, it tried to raise itself up again to this life, but in vain. I was "told" with firm compassion by Him who is nameless that I had had enough, and that it was now right for me to descend into the world of separation, the earth of form and aspiration, to put into practice the teaching that had been given me.

The silent music of eternity gave way to the strains of the "Oberon" overture. I could establish, through my knowledge of the music, that the entire episode had lasted about three minutes. The radiance of the light of eternity was dulled, and was soon replaced by the glow of the electric light bulb in my bedroom. Once more I was at home in bed in my physical body, full of wonder and mute sadness, yet still surrounded by an aura of vibration. This aura persisted for several days, gradually diminishing in intensity, and with it a faint audible vibration that was a distant echo of the celestial sound I had heard during the brief period of illumination.

Over this period I was aware of the peace that passes understanding. I behaved normally, for my general appearance and actions appeared to arouse no special comment. I mention this simply to refute any suggestion of mental disturbance or physical illness as the basis of the remarkable experience I had undergone. In fact I was even brighter mentally after the period of illumination than I had been before, and was to achieve an outstanding result in the matriculation examination at the end of the year. Knowing only too well how little prepared my parents would be for such a disclosure, I purposely refrained from telling them about it. They would either have dismissed it as a dream, or else been seriously worried that I was ailing physically or mentally. Like the mother of Jesus, I stored all these things in my heart, but an inner wisdom kept me from casting them before the profane gaze of the worldly ones.

Jakob Boehme, after his glorious illumination, is reputed as saying that within the space of a quarter of an hour he had learnt more than he would have had he spent many years in a university. In fact, the knowledge that both he and I had been given could never be acquired in any school on this earth. Even those establishments that aspire to occult training teach only the outer form of reality; its core, which is divine love, is as far from its teachers as from the general mass of humanity. God showed me as much of Himself as I could bear to receive: I knew that He is not someone limited as we are. He transcends all categories and is the reality that lies beyond all form, even the whole universe. We can never know Him except in union, when we can receive His outflowing energies: uncreated light that lightens the soul, the mind, and the universe with meaning and purpose; wisdom that informs the creation of the way to fulfilment; love that gives itself unreservedly that the creation may be filled with life and move to completion. It is by love that God comes to us, and in this respect God is personal as well as transpersonal. Love can never fail to be personal when it visits a person, for personality can respond only to personal love.

My obsession about finitude was now relieved. The universe, far from being all that is, is simply the form of reality which we experience in the limitation of time and space. But transcending that form is the eternal realm which was in the beginning, is now, and ever shall be, world without end. The world of form is a world of change, of death, and of becoming. It is penetrated and ultimately transfigured by the uncreated light of God in order to enter into the liberty of eternity where there is no change, but only divine union of such an intensity as to transcend all worldly concepts. "Heaven and earth will pass away, but my words will not pass away" (Mark 13:31).

The infinite preciousness of man's person was also revealed to me: nothing that is created is destroyed by God because of His love for all His creation. Death of the body is merely a state of transition in the development of a soul-filled person. The way of this development is by a rebirth sequence, with immersion in a world of limitation to cause the soul to grow into the knowledge of love. This knowledge comes only with the experience of self-giving service and sacrifice in a world of limited time and space. This rebirth sequence might be an earthly one or else it might occur in some other milieu elsewhere in the universe. It is not an endless circular movement, but rather an ascending spiral one.

I learned that the power of God and the love that flows from it are bestowed equally on all creatures. No particular sect, race, colour, or religious group is either favoured or exempted from that love. It comes to all and sundry as grace when they are ready to receive it. The way of grace is salvation, and all are saved in eternity. There is no wrath in the divine nature but only in the disregarded law that governs the world of limitation in which we have to grow to fullness of being. Without this law there can be no growth. If it is transgressed, as is the rule in the world of sin that we all inherit, suffering is the inevitable result. But the final end of pain is joy and redemption for all who will receive it.

This enlightening knowledge came to me with the experience; it was not deduced intellectually afterwards. The blinding import gave the illumination its awe-inspiring authority.

I have often meditated upon this remarkable revelation, but nothing that I have subsequently read or thought has added to its content or in any way modified it. It has remained the most important event in my life. Even now, more than thirty years later, the memory of it is crystal clear.

It did not prevent me, however, from the experience I was about to endure, the dark night of the soul, when all spiritual light was withheld from me for many years.

4

The Dark Night of the Soul

AFTER THE EXPERIENCE of illumination, I was gradually withdrawn from spiritual things. Instead I had to cope with the process of growing into adult life. The soul, which seemed to have incarnated so imperfectly into the body, had now to make its proper entry and claim its own realm with authority. This was a painful time, and as the process of full incarnation continued, I grew further and further away from spiritual reality. Yet I could never forget what I had been shown, and no matter how much I tried to compromise with the materialistic values that surrounded me, I could never be false to what I knew was the truth. Any submission to values that were false to my inner judgment caused me intense distress and pain.

As I had embarked on a medical career, my attention was fixed emphatically on worldly things. My clumsiness with my hands, in no small measure an inheritance of the sheltered life I had led in which all the menial work had been done by servants, was to some extent ameliorated by dissection and later by examining patients. But I could make no real friends with my fellow students. My only point of contact was intellectual. I could discuss ideas with ease and thereby form a mental relationship with some people considerably older than myself. But my extreme diffidence about my body made any show of physical affection very difficult. I became increasingly inhibited socially, and spent most of my free time in solitude. My scholastic achievements were again in the first rank of excellence, for I could never fail in mental work or in examinations. Indeed, I lived for my work, in which I could, literally, lose myself — and a study of the human body in all its intricacies and excellence is a wonderful theme for perpetual meditation — but I did not know how to spend the holiday periods. Later I worked in hospitals during these times also. In all, I became adept in my work and developed a real passion for the patients I met and for their many problems. But I did not grow into the stature of a man. I was as isolated, as lonely, and as inhibited socially and physically when I qualified as a doctor as I was when I first went to school at the age of five. To enter a shop to buy a simple article was a major trial. An invitation to a party, a rare event in any case since I had so few acquaintances, produced a state of anxiety that half paralysed my faculties for days on end.

I was apt to blame this crippling psychological inhibition on my upbringing. My mother, a fine woman with a noble, upright heart, was neurotically possessive of her only child. Poor woman that she was, for one day the child had to leave her, and progressive mental depression was to be her lot, with death from cancer at too young an age! My father's view of life was shallow and materialistic. Though good and honest in his professional work, he had developed a cynical attitude to the world and saw the selfish part of life as the most real. He distrusted nobility and idealism — and who, surveying the world's progress over the last century, can entirely blame him for this nihilistic view of life? But I can see now that I bore the seeds of my inadequacy within me. I had too strong a character and too powerful a will to be entirely subjugated by any outside influence. While my parents' attitudes were unhelpful in my upbringing, I will always be grateful to them for the beautiful home they provided during the formative years of my childhood, when adverse outer circumstances, such as being incarcerated in a boarding-school, might have crushed me very badly. For the general ethos in those days was much less enlightened than it is today when eccentricity and individuality are much more acceptable in schools, and when the emphasis is less exclusively on physical exercise and more on mental and artistic performance. The whole point of my personal dilemma was that I would not compromise fully with the world around me. Only later was I to learn that I could not so compromise, for this was why I was born as I was.

As I grew older, I saw my contemporaries progressing in their own lives, courting, marrying, and setting up their own homes. Despite my excellent record at the medical school, I had great difficulty in getting the necessary house appointments at the associated hospitals, whereas those whose standard of performance was poor were well installed in these hospitals. It was evident that I was completely lacking in personal assertiveness and aggressiveness, which is a prerequisite for successful material existence. Gradually unpleasant tendencies began to emerge in my own character. The transparent simplicity and joyous wonder of childhood became clouded with feelings of jealousy, resentment, and vague fear. I began, quite involuntarily, to gloat over any disappointment in the life of a contemporary and to wish that any possible happiness, such as an impending marriage, might be thwarted. A tendency to make mischief showed itself, and I felt increasingly resentful of my own inhibited personality which was robbing me of the comforts and social achievements of others. And yet, in my deepest awareness, I had no real desire either for marriage or for material prosperity. When I was a small child I had already understood the futility of worldly riches: in my imagination I could be the richest, the most powerful, the most awe-inspiring man in the world. After about five minutes this model of earthly desire became nauseatingly boring, and I was happy to let it go. I knew, even at that age, love is alone worth having, and this knowledge never left me, even in my periods of greatest despair.

In 1951 I left South Africa and settled in Britain for postgraduate medical training. I knew intuitively that I would never return to live in my native land, for my horizons could not be enclosed in a community that practised racial discrimination. I also knew that the parting of the ways with my parents was close at hand. The time drew near when I had to bid farewell to the house where I had spent my prophetic childhood. That home alone knew my innermost secrets; it had been the place where Christ revealed Himself to me and instructed me how I should live. In it the supreme illumination of the Godhead had been given me through divine grace. I had confided my highest aspirations to its walls, and the depths of my fears were known in its rooms. In the garden I had paced out my meditations. It alone really knew me; every piece of furniture was a blessed friend. And now it was to fade from visible view forever. But in my dreams it is never far from me, and I have no doubt I will visit it once more in the form of mental reality when I have quitted the body of humiliation and put on the body of spiritual light.

My parents accompanied me to Europe, and after a short holiday together, they left me to return to South Africa. The final parting was mutely poignant. I knew how my mother was gradually breaking down inwardly as the day of departure drew nearer. At last the taxi arrived to carry them both to the air terminal, and I saw their well-remembered faces for the last time as they disappeared into the distance. I was to see them together on only one subsequent visit three years later, when the decline in my mother's health was already apparent. Soon afterwards her final illness struck. Against my father there was a feeling of mounting hostility that eventually culminated in a healing hatred. This strange description of hatred must shock the more conventional reader, but I was later to learn that a fully acknowledged hatred is the beginning of a future understanding that may, with God's help, flower into real compassion and love. It is the cold indifference of so many relationships, masked by superficial politeness and calculated urbanity, that is the true cancer of the personality. Schools of religious and metaphysical thought that refuse to face the fact of hostility, war, and evil are also unable to redeem these unpleasant ingredients of earthly life. They exist in us and around us whether we accept them intellectually or not. If we make them our own, they can be redeemed by the love of God; if we ignore them they will possess us and lead to enormous destruction. The God who created light also created darkness (Genesis 1:1-5). Both material light and darkness must be transfigured by the uncreated light of God that flows from His Spirit through receptive human beings.

My life in England was very different from that which I had known in South Africa. There were no servants and no parents. I was completely alone, and had now, for the first time in my life, to fend for myself. I had indeed been thrown in at the deep end, but was able to adapt to the changed circumstances extremely well. There was only one thing that could not be changed, my own personality. The sense of strangeness and the inability to communicate with those around me, except in intellectual precepts, persisted. My social inhibitions increased in intensity. At first I was able to lose myself in medical study preliminary to taking postgraduate examinations, which I, as usual, passed successfully at the first attempt. But when I had achieved all I could professionally, I was bereft and alone. Once again the inability to assert myself prevented my acquiring the type of hospital appointment that would have been commensurate with my medical knowledge, added to which there was the handicap of being an outsider and so having no personal backing from influential colleagues. Nevertheless, considering the severe psychological difficulty under which I laboured, it is remarkable that I achieved what I did professionally. I was never out of work, and was highly esteemed by my colleagues on a professional level even if there was no effective social relationship between us.

During this dark period I sometimes lived alone in a bed-sitting room, and sometimes in a hospital mess. I preferred the latter, for I enjoyed the company of my fellows and never really chose solitude. This fact was of great inner reassurance, for it indicated to me that my social sense was basically normal and that there was no serious mental disturbance at the root of my difficulties. Indeed, ordinary social intercourse in a friendly, co-operative atmosphere was a great joy to me; it was only when some outside event, like Christmas festivities with their surfeit of over-drinking and excessive social fraternisation, loomed large that my inhibitions mounted and I disappeared into a quiet corner. During this period I had to undertake two years of compulsory military service. The threat of this overshadowed my life for many months beforehand, but when at last the time came, I found the experience far more agreeable than I could have imagined. I spent most of this period overseas in Nigeria and Cyprus where I learnt much both medically and sociologically, but once again there was no really deep communication with any of my colleagues. It was obvious that I could not release myself properly, while they, quite properly, were much more concerned with their private family attachments.

When I had completed my military service and had returned to civilian life, I was thrown firmly on my own resources. There was to be no more communal life, but only a private detached existence. No longer could I lose myself in group activities; I had to face my dereliction and ask myself what life was really about, and what I hoped to achieve. I had by this time become a university lecturer, and it became clear to me that I would never ascend far up the academic ladder: my social inhibitions would bar any significant promotion. The spiritual darkness, which had closed in on me progressively since the age of sixteen, was now almost impenetrable. I was filled with intense, though ill-defined, fear. My contact with spiritual reality was tenuous, and my prayer life, which had once been a spontaneous outflowing of joy to God the Creator, was now a mere gasp in the overwhelming ocean of dark meaninglessness. I was running desperately hard, but there was no clear destination. I longed to be safe at home, but there was no home, only a place of uneasy rest. The years were passing by, and having achieved all I could intellectually, I knew that I had achieved nothing at all. I was enclosed in a fog of incomprehension; those around me were pleasant and kindly, but they could not help for they did not understand. The only purpose in life was to keep on living. The fear of annihilation was the impetus that kept me in my professional work, and an obsessional drive to technical perfection made my life bearable. But I had no basis for living. In fact, I was experiencing the dark night of the soul.

To come to some social reality, I tried desperately hard to be sociable, to speak enthusiastically about nothing in particular. But all that came of this was a tendency to disparage others and to speak scandal, which often passes for wit in shallow society. When I saw what I was doing I became ashamed of myself, and crept further into my shell. Inhibition was preferable to false conviviality. Loneliness was more palatable than forced sociability. What I did not know then was that those around me who appeared socially at ease and full of self-confidence were also in hell, but were unaware of it. They concealed their own rootlessness, even with home and family, in a show of urbanity and good living.

The abyss of meaninglessness lay in front of us all, but I, with my heightened spiritual perception, could see it, whereas they were blinded by material delusion.

5

The Dawning of the Light

MATTERS FINALLY REACHED a head when I had to start lecturing to postgraduate students in a large hall. I was extremely happy teaching them, but was quite incapable of raising my voice sufficiently to be heard even in the close confines of a room. I went to a fine speech therapist, who at once diagnosed the difficulty as a spasm of the muscles of the larynx, a spasm elicited by fear and anxiety. In other words, my difficulty was fundamentally psychological. She taught me how to relax and breathe properly with the diaphragm, so that within a remarkably short time I had overcome the vocal trouble and could speak loudly and audibly even in a large lecture theatre.

It was evident, however, that the inability to raise my voice was merely a symptom of a much deeper psychological disturbance, and the therapist, who herself had had emotional problems that had been helped by a psychiatrist, urged me likewise to seek help. I hesitated at this suggestion; I had already read some of the writings of the exponents of psycho-analysis and behaviour therapy, and these had distressed me. The agnosticism about spiritual experience and the general contempt for religious values that most of these writers expressed troubled me. I knew how easy it would be to explain away the deep inner experiences of earlier years as episodes of wishful thinking and escape from an intolerably lonely childhood: what I had failed to achieve on a material level could be actualised in dramatic private fantasies. And yet I knew with absolute certainty that those experiences had been the most real part of my life; if they were taken away, whatever meaning my existence held would be lost.

It so happened that a girl who lived in the same house as I told me, quite unexpectedly, about a course in psychology that was being conducted nearby under the auspices of the London County Council (as it was then called). She had found the content of these lectures helpful, and so I went myself to listen, hoping that these might form an acceptable introduction to psychotherapy. I expected a well-qualified psychologist replete with diplomas and possibly having psycho-analytic experience giving drily expert advice about emotional troubles. Instead I was confronted by a stout elderly woman who did not use the language of academic psychology, but spoke instead about the proper inner development of the complete person. She described the inner life, not with the detached agnosticism of the professional psychologist, but with a loving reverence that testified to her own experience and wisdom. I soon found that she had no degrees and diplomas; in more normal circumstances, I, a well-qualified young medical practitioner, might have dismissed her as a crank who taught "popular psychology." But my need had brought me to the abyss of humility, and I was prepared to listen to a wisdom that was not academic or learned, but came instead from the life experience of a very remarkable person. She was not ignorant of the theories of the three leading psycho-analysts — Freud, Jung, and Adler — and had indeed much respect for their insights, especially those of Jung, but her breadth of thought embraced such themes as ultimate meaning of life, the supremacy of the soul, and the fact of God. At once I realised I was in the presence of a person I really knew, and could at last start being myself after sixteen years in the wilderness — for the dark night of the soul had lasted exactly the same period of time as had my childhood which culminated in the great mystical experience that I described in a previous chapter.

Soon themes that were buried deep in my mind but had seldom been brought into the light of day were openly discussed: the properties of the soul and its probable pre-existence of the body that enclosed it, the phenomenon of rebirth in a succession of lives, and the possibility of reincarnation.

Reincarnation is a concept that still strikes horror in the hearts of many Western people, who confuse it with the transmigration of souls into the bodies of animals. In fact, it is a very reasonable way of envisaging the experience and growth of the soul in a series of human bodies, and as such is accepted in the Hindu-Buddhist tradition. That this hypothesis has some factual basis has been shown by recent psychical research into the astounding prenatal memories — which have been confirmed — of very small children, too young to have acquired the knowledge from any person living in their vicinity. The fact of rebirth was shown unequivocally to me during the illuminative experience I have already described, but I was not given any indication about the frequency of a return to earthly conditions.

Thus I began to unburden myself of the knowledge that lay deep within me, but which I had previously protected from the destructive gaze of the ignorantly hostile. At last, sixteen years after the event, I could discuss my great mystical experience with a sympathetic person; indeed, for the first time in my life I had a real conversation about the profound issues of existence. Soon I met others who had also attended this course of lectures — which were suitably entitled "Understanding Ourselves" — and at last I began to move freely amongst people with whom I could converse with ease. My loneliness was at an end.

The important fact that emerged from this encounter and the subsequent course of my life was that there was nothing essentially wrong with me mentally or emotionally. I was certainly an unusual type of person — and who, in his own way, is completely devoid of unusual characteristics? But there was nothing intrinsically abnormal about me. The psychological difficulties were the result of involuntary attempts at suppressing my true nature and conforming slavishly to the standards of the world. My case was comparable with that of a person with exceptionally fine vision who tries to view his surroundings with spectacles designed for one that is very short-sighted, and who even pretends to the world that the result is pleasant. Once I came to myself I could at last begin to relax. What I had to do was to return to the inner completeness of my early childhood, but with the wisdom and compassion that had accrued from my experience in the world.

As my inner condition fell more into place, a considerable amount of aggressiveness was released, and most of this was visited on my poor father to whom I wrote a series of unpleasant, though distinctly pertinent letters. It was to take seven years before the light of God's forgiveness healed my own soul, after which a reconciliation with my father at last became possible. It was good that, even during the worst of the bitterness, we never lost contact with each other. Apart from this one lamentable, though necessary episode, my reactive aggressiveness was channelled into more constructive work.

What I had been given through the grace of God had now to be transmitted to others. Both the inner revelations and the outer suffering I had endured were to be fertilised in service to those on the path of self-realisation. It was interesting that a weak voice had led to my final liberation; that same voice, now firm and assured, was to be the principal means of liberating others from the shackles of meaninglessness and fear. Later the pen was to supplement the spoken word, so that the message could go out further afield.

Two spiritual gifts showed themselves almost as soon as I came to myself, as the beautiful Parable of the Prodigal Son puts it. The first was an ability to reach a state of formless contemplation at will. I was concentrating on everyday questions, like "How are you?" or "What is the time?" repeated over and over again without an answer. Suddenly I became aware of the silence, a mere second that elapsed between the conclusion of the question and its repetition. That silence was more eloquent than the words which encompassed it, for in the silence I was aware of the eternal life lifting up the world and giving it meaning. As soon as I became aware of the reality of that momentary silence, I could attain it at will and remain in it indefinitely. Of course, I now realise that what, on the face of it, sounds a childishly simple exercise may need the work of a lifetime. I myself needed all the previous understanding I had to attain it, and its attainment was God-given as well as self-achieved.

In this silence my psychic powers, latent for the last sixteen years, were once again activated. I became aware of other people's inner needs and dispositions, and I could sense with remarkable accuracy the presence of evil in an environment. At one time I might have discounted such extrasensory — or perhaps I should rather say higher sensory — information, but my disillusionment with the narrow limits of knowledge set by conventional scientific philosophy made me less sceptical and more willing to accept these hidden sources of knowledge. On the other hand, my critical intelligence and scientific training prevented me falling into the morass of credulity that so often bedevils amateur enthusiasts of psychical research. On more than one occasion, when my mind was quiet and untroubled, I was aware of mental communication with friends who had died and were now living in the greater life beyond the grave. Sometimes the messages were emotional and loving, but therefore less evidential.

The second gift, which was directly related to the first, was that of spontaneous spiritual utterance of such a calibre that I was soon able to deliver completely unprepared addresses and lectures, lasting up to an hour on some occasions. When I reached the silence and lifted up my soul to God in prayer, His Holy Spirit descended on me, and I started to speak with an authority and an eloquence far outside my usual range. And yet I was in complete control; my state of consciousness was raised, and I had lost all self-concern or self-consciousness. It was as if the Holy Spirit was speaking through me, and using the great store-house of wisdom and experience that my educated, sensitive mind had accumulated during the painful process of its growth. In other words, the addresses were of a completely different order from the boring, platitudinous utterances that Spiritualist mediums in the dissociated state of trance so often deliver. At first I used to prepare notes beforehand, but when the time for speaking arrived, I found that the written word interfered with the spontaneous communication that passed between me and the audience. It required great faith to dispense with all such preparations and depend entirely upon God for inspiration, but once this had been attained, I never doubted the source of inspiration and relied on it absolutely. My particular qualifications for this gift appeared to be a well-educated mind with much experience of the inner life and a selfless concern for those who were listening. This selflessness was the result of the harrowing period in the wilderness that I had undergone. All concern for self-inflation ceased after the private self had been destroyed in the refining fire of suffering. If I had ever used the gift to impress myself on others, it would soon have left me, and my address would have descended to the level of a personal display designed to win applause.

It took five years of preparation from the time of restoration of spiritual light for me to be properly equipped for my particular ministry. My shyness and social ineptitude did not evaporate immediately — indeed, in a very real way I still bear their impress — but they ceased to cripple me. Instead I was able to use them to effect a close relationship with unhappy distraught people who could never have tolerated the smooth urbanity of an unwounded, insensitive therapist. The intense sensitivity that had always been my lot, while making me particularly helpful to those in need, also rendered me abnormally vulnerable to both the open insult and the hidden hostility of others. This was why I had to boost my morale with brilliant examination results in my youth. Now that I had to give of myself in word to the world, a terrible fear of publicity and the consequent loss of privacy assailed me. At first I could hardly bear to hear my name mentioned in public, and I took great care to conceal all my private interests lest they would damage my professional career. But as the years passed, I became less obsessed with my own safety and put the work with greater faith into the hands of the Holy Spirit.

While these changes were occurring on an inner level, and I was venturing into contemplative prayer, my professional life blossomed into much more interesting activities. My proficiency as a teacher and lecturer, itself in no small measure the fruit of the sessions with the speech therapist, enabled me to relate more closely with the students and my colleagues. It was unfortunate that at this time internecine strife broke out in the place where I worked. This was due, as is so often the case in this type of situation, to a clash of personalities involving some of my colleagues. Though I was not in the first case directly involved, there came a time in which I had to stand up and be counted among those whom I considered to be in the right. The result of this, as might be expected, was that my professional career was blighted and all hope of promotion blocked. I, nevertheless, in collaboration with a fellow lecturer, wrote a text-book which, much to our surprise, was destined to become a best-seller. However, the frustration of my academic ambitions and the terrible atmosphere under which I worked was a hard burden to bear. This unpleasant state of affairs lasted nine years before the person most responsible for the trouble suddenly left and moved elsewhere. On the surface this would have seemed a well nigh impossible event.

I mention this distasteful episode to emphasise that a proper spiritual perspective, far from rendering one less fit for the hardships of worldly life, aids in concentrating one's inner resources and making one cope far better than would otherwise have been possible. In this we see an important quality of true spirituality: it leads one on to a more fruitful life on earth. On more than one occasion I was tempted to quit my position and move elsewhere, but each time my sense of personal grievance was overridden by the strength of my spiritual vocation, which I knew had to be pursued in the place where I was living.

Even when I was a child I seemed to have a premonition of later frustration, and I had a persistent fear of being left out of the world's race. It was this that surely acted as the motive for my obsessional striving for scholastic excellence. Later I came to understand that the frustration which I experienced in my earlier adult life was a necessary corrective for my immature, selfish approach to life. I had to learn patience in the course of delay, forbearance towards inadequate people whose selfish actions caused general havoc, and longsuffering during the course of personal injustice. Now I know that only by suffering long does one learn to love others and become proficient in life.

During an early period of this phase of my life, I had a prophetic dream which has been progressively fulfilled: I was walking down a sordid side-street in the city of my birth, when I suddenly fell into an open manhole and descended into a subterranean cavern. It was not an ordinary enclosed cavern, but instead extended in long corridors under the earth.

These passages were dark and repulsive, but as I walked down them they seemed to open up into wider, barely separate rooms which were poorly lit. In these rooms there were all manner of people pursuing drab occupations, and eventually I found myself in a room in which there was a central operating table. The other people there were ill-defined, but presumably had some connexion with the healing profession. I was taught with great perseverance, the rudiments of physical therapy — for as always my physical equipment was clumsy and unsure — until the time came when I had learned a great deal about the body.

One of the surly, but not unkind men in this subterranean room then told me that I had learned all that they could teach me, and that the time had come to re-enter the world again. I then ascended from the depths by a small hole on to the surface once more. The locality was a different part of the same city where I had been walking at the beginning of the dream. It too was not a particularly pleasant district, but the sun was shining wanly through dissipating clouds, and I knew I had to progress onwards into the distance where there was a hint of promise.

6

The Testing of Spirits

FROM THE SMALL group of people that gravitated around the teacher of self-understanding who restored the light of spiritual day to me, I was to make contact with an ever-widening circle of acquaintances, some of whom were to become firm friends. I soon became aware that my path was not, indeed never had been, random or fortuitous, but was being directed by a power far beyond the strength of my own will. To be sure, I had the choice of rejecting this higher direction, but as I grew more fully into a real person, so I accepted this higher impulse and actively co-operated with it.

This is, in fact, the meaning of free will. In one respect we are never free, for if we live in a state of complete licence and anarchy, we soon come to disintegration and destruction. We can either conform to the lower law of worldly society, and gather in the immediate benefits and later sufferings, or else we can become obedient to God and give ourselves entirely to His service. It is this service which, paradoxically, is the meaning of true freedom, for having transcended the thraldom of the personality, we are now living the eternal life of the true self, or soul. The servant of God does not divorce himself from worldly society and its law; on the contrary, he co-operates joyously with it, in order not merely to benefit from it, but also to redeem it. Christ's admonition to render unto Caesar the things that are Caesar's, and to God the things that are God's follows from this. Even the works of Caesar are given by God, and are finally subordinate to Him. When St. Paul could describe himself as an apostle of Christ, he was free even during the periods of intense suffering.

The path I was to follow, as I knew even in my childhood, was one to a knowledge of God. The mystical experience I had as a youth was both the consummation of my childhood aspirations and the confirmation for the work that lay ahead. The prolonged period of darkness was a time of testing. I survived by faith, sometimes against all faith, and proved conclusively to myself that spiritual values were the most real aspects of existence. I had to learn to co-operate with the powers of this world, but I could not conform to them. St. Paul puts this very well. He says: "Be not conformed to this world, but be ye transformed by the renewing of your mind, that ye may prove what is that good, and acceptable, and perfect, will of God" (Romans 12:22). It is, as he points out, by the remaking of the mind and the consequent transformation of the whole nature that one can discern God's will and know what is right. This remaking of man in the divine image can be initiated and executed by God alone, but only with the full, unstinted co-operation of man. The gift of free will, man's most priceless personal possession, ensures that God Himself cannot — and indeed will not — trespass on the holy ground that He Himself has bequeathed to man, until man bids Him enter. But when He does enter there is a reforming of the whole personality, which entails a prior demolition of much that was regarded as sacrosanct to man's well-being. And if He is then repudiated, there is terrible suffering. No wonder it is a fearful thing to fall into the hands of the living God (Hebrews 10:31).

The circle of people I now associated with — and they grew progressively in number as one introduced me to another — were all seeking actively for God, though most of them would not have seen their endeavours in such stark relief. They wanted answers to their particular difficulties, and had had enough bitter experience to realise that the orthodox sources of enlightenment — the medical profession and the Church — were of little use to them in their searching.

I myself was brought up in the Jewish faith, but in its liberal rather than its orthodox tradition. My parents could hardly be described as devout religionists, but we did at least observe the most important holidays. Synagogue worship was a joy to me, and I was well aware of the presence of God when the sacred Scroll of the Law was presented, unrolled, and read during the most holy part of the service. I am very grateful that I was brought up in the Jewish religion, which I still regard as the central manifestation and guardian of God's self-revelation to man. Never at any time did I submit to the temptation of changing my name with its obvious religious overtones, for I knew that both its glory and its burden were part of my heritage, and one that had to be both acknowledged and redeemed. In fact I suffered minimally from anti-Semitic prejudice, unlike my unfortunate relatives in Lithuania, all of whom were burnt alive in their village synagogue by the Nazis during the early part of the Russian campaign.

And yet Christ disclosed Himself to me when I was scarcely out of infancy. I could never escape from Him even had I been so inclined. I began to see Him both as the consummation of all that Judaism had taught and witnessed, and also the power of God universalised to all men, of all races. I knew that, though He was a man as I was, in Him the power of God shone eternally, and He was in His life and witness to the truth, the manifestation of the one God in the flesh. He had fulfilled the universalisation of Judaism to which the Prophets had looked forward. From all this I deduced that God was greater than the Jewish religion, and in Christ was available to all people. A restricted, racially orientated view of election and salvation was not sufficient. No one group of people was specially selected for God's love or favour. My illumination made this fact absolutely clear.

But what about Christianity, the religion that had arisen as a direct result of the incarnation of Jesus Christ, and had eclipsed its mother Judaism? Logically I should have sought admission within its portals as soon as I was independent of my parents. But I discovered, very soon, that this too was no divinely inspired religion. Even when a child in South Africa, I met enough Christians to see that their religion did not appear to bear any great impress of holiness. They were selfish, racialistic, mean, and as dishonest in their personal relationships as those who did not profess a religious belief. Indeed, if anything they were rather worse, because their religion produced a veneer of sanctimonious piety that drew out their deeper spiritual deficiency. I must confess that the Christian religion that I observed in my youth was not an attractive proposition for anyone contemplating the spiritual path. Its Catholic exponents were arrogant and triumphalistic, while the Evangelical groups preached a doctrine that damned man and dishonoured God, who was made to resemble a ferocious tyrant rather than the Lord of love. I personally could never be other than liberal in my religious views, but my liberalism was mystically inspired and not rationalistic. And mystical awareness, I was to find, is a rare commodity amongst Western religionists, whether Jew or Christian.

A sweeping denunciation of the type of Christianity I observed in my youth is bound to be unjust. Amongst the indifferent mass of Christians who lorded it over the lesser breeds, there were truly saintly people whose lives were devoted to the service of others, and courageous priests who, at great personal peril, denounced racial injustice and cruelty. But these were voices crying out in the wilderness; the flock were at best ambivalent in their response to their pastors. This local situation mirrored that occurring in Germany at the same period. The main churches played a sinister role in the triumph of Nazism, largely through their innate anti-Semitic bias, and even at the worst period of terror, their witness was ambivalent despite the self-sacrifice of a few really great Christians.

From all this I learned that Christ was far greater than the Church that had arisen in His name. He is the power, the light that enlightens every man, which moves all men on from the lesser to the greater, from the personal self to the spiritual self where God is known, and where Christ dwells and His Spirit sanctifies the whole personality. The reverse side of this spiritual truth, the importance of the Christian Church, was hidden from me at this stage. I was later to come to this understanding also.

During the dark period of my life when I came to England, I finally broke with traditional Judaism; a complete stranger, I now chose my own way of life, and moved as I wished. The main churches were unhelpful, for the religious atmosphere of the Fifties I found to be self-assured and triumphalistic. The break-through into real religious awareness came, significantly, from the Roman Catholic Church, previously the most reactionary, recalcitrant, and triumphalistic of all the churches, through two great personalities, Pope John XXIII and Pierre Teilhard de Chardin. The former was to humanise his church during his short period of office, and to replace triumphalistic assurance with humble service in the steps of the Master. Teilhard, despite the limitations of his perspective, which was mystical rather than truly scientific, laid the foundations of an authentically humanistic Christianity that saw Christ as the very process of evolution to that far off day envisaged by St. Paul, when the universe was to be freed from the shackles of mortality and enter upon the liberty and splendour of the children of God (Romans 8:21). At last the church was being shaken to its foundations, and was no longer merely the repository of dead tradition.

It was in this changing atmosphere that I at last emerged from the shadows. Radical religious thought was in the air, and many of the past assumptions were being openly questioned. I myself joined a non-credal liberal Christian group whose basis of belief was rationalistic. Its members did not accept the divinity of Christ, but followed Him as a great ethical teacher and exemplar. Likewise they dismissed the "supernatural" part of the Gospel, including the healing miracles, as relics of past ignorance, now mercifully superseded by the all-encompassing wisdom of modern science. Despite the obvious deficiency of this presentation of the Christian faith, I am grateful for my stay with this group. Their intellectual honesty was refreshing and enlightening, and there were moments of great depth in our worship when the desiccating intellect could be stilled in a brief, but eloquent silence. I soon realised that when the divinity is taken away from Christ and He is put in His place as one of many great human teachers, He becomes increasingly unnecessary to us. Likewise, the intellect that can dismiss all aspects of life that fall outside current scientific thinking as unreal or meaningless, can soon demolish the concept of God. Such rationalistic religious liberalism tends to move progressingly towards atheistic humanism. And I could never be a humanist, much as I respect the courage and intellectual integrity of the ethically based non-believer. The root defect in the rationalistic view of reality is a failure in imagination.

Fortunately my spiritual diet did not consist only of rationalistic Christianity. The people with whom I had most in common had, as I have already noted, a yearning to know the true God, who did not seem to reveal Himself in the mainstream churches or to be found in books of philosophy or psychology. Many of them had had transient psychical experiences, and a few had even had a glimpse of the greater reality of mysticism. Few were completely balanced emotionally, and few were intellectually proficient. The contrast between them and the rationalists could hardly have been more stark, but they shared one quality: a dissatisfaction with conventional credal religion and a passionate desire to find a deeper meaning to life than the mere repetition of surface activities from day to day until the time of death. It was inevitable that this group of people should follow the non-rational path to reality. Their interest in psychism led them either into spiritualistic groups or else into the more pretentious schools of theosophical thought that had their basis in the writings of H. P. Blavatsky and her numerous successors. A few were anthroposophists, followers of that remarkable seer Rudolf Steiner, while others followed the teachings of the schools of New Thought, the basis of which was that, by thinking positively, our lives could be changed and all manner of good things come to us. Some of the more powerful personalities were attracted to the self-realisation philosophies of Gurdjieff and his pupil P.D. Ouspensky.

It seems that I was taken, under the auspices of the Holy Spirit, on a short visit to these various outposts of the occult, in order to understand their attractions and to discern their over-all inadequacy in fostering true spirituality. It was at that time that the concept of a "New Age" was becoming current amongst many younger, more mystically aware people. This "New Age" was linked closely to the constellation Aquarius under whose astrological influence the earth was now beginning to move. Aquarius, the water-carrier, symbolised the down-pouring of cosmic energies on to our planet, and these forces would inspire receptive, open-minded people to psychical and mystical realisation. The rigidity of the past would be superseded by a Spirit-filled generation that would, like the earliest Christians, turn the world upside down. All this was very exciting, and I believe contained more than a germ of truth. Certainly there are strong psychical forces at work in the world now; the Charismatic Renewal in the churches, itself an ambivalent manifestation, is one aspect of this power, but so also are the menacing social and political upheavals that are now an every-day event even in previously stable societies. It is evident that not every psychical current is divine; quite a proportion of psychical manifestations are demonic.

My first impression of non-rational (which is not the same as irrational) occult teaching was favourable. It was apparently open, non-credal, universalistic in scope, and knowledgeable about the deeper aspects of reality, including the life of the soul after death of the physical body. Much of what had been revealed to me was taught by practitioners of these schools of thought. At last I seemed to be in the right milieu. But soon my inner discernment bade me beware. The surface was plausible enough, but the under-currents were treacherous.

I found that advocates of spiritualistic communication with the unseen world through mediums, or sensitives, did not grow into fullness of being. Having jettisoned the authority of the Bible or the Church, they had merely bound themselves to the voice of the medium through whom a "control", or "guide" (often with a Red-Indian name), spoke. The teachings varied much in quality. Being only on the periphery of Spiritualism, I did not come across anything very disturbing, but I was soon aware of the prosaic, platitudinous quality of even the higher teachings.

The nature of a spiritualistic guide is itself questionable; is it merely a part if the medium's personality that has split off and acquired autonomy, or is it a discarnate source from the formless world beyond the grave? And, above all, by what authority does it teach and give advice? Whatever the answers to these questions, it became evident to me that there was far too close a dependence of many Spiritualists on the advice of the guide. They had substituted a psychic source of authority for a religious one, and no matter how sincere its teaching, they were not growing fully as persons. Many went for advice about mundane matters to these sources, so that their own powers of judgment were gradually weakened. It was accepted that direct communication occurred frequently between the living and the dead through the medium and his (or more often her) guide. My own investigations, aided by the power of spiritual discernment, suggested that on some occasions this claim was justified, but by far the majority of communications were simple mind-reading exercises by the medium, who gave the sitter the information he unconsciously desired. This was no conscious fraud on the part of the medium, who was in my experience a dedicated, sympathetic person, but simply an aspect of the treacherous terrain of the psychic world. The phenomena of extrasensory perception, of which I had had much experience in my own life, were shown to me, as a detached, objective observer, to be real and fully deserving specialised investigation by competent psychical research workers. But as a way of life and a guide to God they were illusory. Psychical understanding illuminated some of the more obscure episodes of the Bible, especially the amazing gifts of Jesus and those who had preceded and followed Him, but in themselves they led merely to self-inflation and delusion.

The psychic path comes to a dead-end. It substitutes meretricious phenomena for God-inspired love in action and self-inflating sensations for the peace that passes understanding.

My contact with various theosophical schools similarly revealed conflicting currents. Much of the basic teachings hailed from Hindu, and to a lesser extent Buddhist sources. This in itself was unexceptionable, but on this scheme of the perennial philosophy there were grafted esoteric systems of thought allegedly derived from high sources, or "Masters" as they were called, which infused the elect with a special aura of superiority. They were the ones who knew. They had many

answers to life and death; the scheme of reincarnation was open
to them; and they spoke with great authority about their
previous lives on earth. Though I was myself very sympathetic
to the concept of reincarnation, as I have already said, this
mechanical view of life and its recurring round of rebirth
according to past actions, or "karma", without the fertilising
power of love to redeem it, troubled me. I could not find the
love of Christ in this scheme — although Jesus was assuredly
included as one of the "Masters". There was much in
theosophical teaching that reminded me of the gnostic sects
that so troubled the early Fathers of the Christian Church.
There was an escape from the sordidness of the world into a
realm of spiritual enlightenment presided over by persons who
"knew". Salvation was linked to self-attained knowledge. A
knowledge of God, however, comes not by esoteric wisdom but
by love. I found much in theosophical teachings of interest and
some of importance, but by itself, this approach comes to
another dead-end. This was also my conclusion about anthro-
posophy, which hung on the teachings of Rudolf Steiner. Some
anthroposophists did wonderful educational and remedial work
amongst the mentally handicapped and the crippled. They
were, of all students of the occult, the nearest to the heart of
Christ. On the other hand, their strongly gnostic affinities led
to exclusiveness and isolation.

My impression of New Thought groups was also mixed.
While it is certainly better to take an optimistic view of the
situation that confronts one than be pessimistic about it, and to
see the bright side of all circumstances rather than the dark,
one should not blind oneself to the darkness and evil in the
world and also in oneself. While it may be possible, by
concentrated powerful thought, to influence situations and
people to one's own advantage, it is doubtful whether the
benefits that follow are either long-lasting or even good for
one's proper growth. Since the beginning of his conscious life,
man has sought after magical means of overcoming his
difficulties. The psychic path often leads to a dependence on
magic, which is the employment of "occult" forces to influence
the physical world to the advantage of the practitioner. Such
attempts, even if they are well intentioned initially, invariably

become demonic, or "black", and the power injures both the object and the agent.

A rather similar criticism applied to many schools of character development and self-realisation that I investigated: their basis was selfish and grasping. Submission to God and the experience of grace in the downflow of the Holy Spirit, Who alone heals and sanctifies, were absent from these systems that relied entirely on man's own abilities. Some groups stressed a conditional immortality dependent on the amount of personal growth one had achieved in this life. The all-embracing, welcoming love of God — as typified in the Parable of the Prodigal Son — was not included in this philosophy. The loveless rigidity and self-consciousness of some of these groups were all too obvious to behold. Their spontaneity seemed to have been destroyed, and there was no real communication between the members and other people. All were intent on self-mastery, and there was no compassion or love for others.

It was evident that I would find no home in this confused mass of esoteric thought. If I had to summarise the essential failing of both the rationalist and the esoteric seekers after wisdom, it would be that neither could be receptive to divine grace. Each had to be doing or learning something for his own growth. Neither had learned that true wisdom comes from within, not through grasping but by waiting patiently on God in prayer. A divine ignorance is the portal to divine knowledge, the knowledge of the love of God.

On the other hand, I also found much of value in my occult studies. Psychic communication is a fact, and it extends both among the living and those who have died. I knew this already from the experience of my own silence, and it was confirmed in my studies of Spiritualism. Personally I deprecate indiscriminate communication with the unseen, and believe mediumship should be reserved for scientific study. But I have no doubt that as one progresses in spiritual stature, so one can communicate far more effectively both with those living around one and with .those who have departed this world. I hope that this type of communion, which is always initiated by the deceased, will be of more frequent occurrence in the future.

I have much less confidence in the thrusting type of communication initiated by the bereaved through the agency of mediums. Here delusion is much more likely.

The teachings of the theosophical schools also shed light on the continuity of life, even if their scheme is too assured and dogmatic. I dislike the emphasis on "Masters", who tend to assume the potentialities of gods. But who can deny the possibility that the Holy Spirit works through the whole communion of saints, of which we all, both in the flesh and in the world beyond death, are members? Amongst "all the company of heaven" may there not be advanced souls (the spirits of just men made perfect — Hebrews 12:23) helping the world to grow into divine understanding? Perhaps this is the most valuable insight that both Spiritualism and Theosophy have to offer us, even if we may disagree with some of their practices and assumptions.

Of the importance of thinking about uplifting things St. Paul says, "Whatsoever things are true...honourable...just...pure ...lovely...of good report; if there be any virtue, and if there be any praise, think on these things" (Philippians 4:8). This is real positive thinking. It moves towards the searching honesty of the intellectually proficient as well as the beauty of the aesthetically pure. The spiritual life also needs an assiduous inner discipline, not so very different from some of the techniques taught by schools of self-realisation. But the aim is to make the person a better servant of God — which entails the humility and simplicity of a child — and not simply more full of power and dynamic magnetism.

The occultist's approach to spirituality is often very close to the true article. No wonder it is said that false Christs and false prophets shall rise, and shall show signs and wonders, to seduce, if it were possible, even the elect (Mark 13:22). But there is one certain sign of the true prophet — a burning love of such a kind that he does not hesitate to give up his life for mankind.

7

A Return to the Roots

MY INVESTIGATION INTO occult teaching had the important result of leading me to a wider grasp of Eastern religious thought. To compare the type of literature that I had perused with the Eastern scriptures was to contrast the stuffy air of a humid room with the vast fragrance of a spring landscape. I exulted in the mental freedom and mystical beauty of the Upanishads and Bhagavadgita of Hinduism, the Buddhist Dhammapada, and the Tao Teh King of Lao Tzu. The overwhelming spaciousness of the Gita was the verbal counterpart of my great mystical experience; it was free and vibrant with life. To this day the Bhagavadgita has remained my favourite book with the sole exception of the Bible.

Eastern religion has long practised the deep inner silence, and in consequence can co-operate with the forces of life by waiting in patience. It is not limited by concepts of time or space, but is aware of eternity, a state that transcends the flux of the world we live in. As a result it has achieved a tranquillity and rest that are far removed from the obsessive concern for outer action that characterises the West. There is a breadth and tolerance in the pages of the Gita that have no equal in any Western text. As a result Eastern religion has little desire to convert others to its view; it is aware that each person is fulfilling his own destiny according to his own pattern of life and the gifts native to him.

But this expansive timeless tolerance also has its limitations. It has little concern for history, and it deals with exalted intellectual concepts rather than with finite people. Eastern religion has so deep a grasp of man's inner psychology that the West seems by contrast merely to skim the surface. But there is correspondingly less concern in the East about social justice and the proper husbanding of the earth. It became evident to me that the spirit of Christ illuminates the whole scheme of Eastern religious thought, but He did not effectively enter the world through it. In other words, the incarnation of Christ and its redeeming effect on the whole created universe was untouched in this approach to reality. The result was the witness of isolated saints who had attained the acme of spiritual illumination surrounded by a mass of countless unenlightened people, many of whom lived in the most appalling poverty and squalor. I began to understand how much East and West needed each other's insights. The West needed the Hindu-Buddhists' emphasis of inner development, especially the practice of contemplation, whereas the East desperately required an incarnational theology to lift up the earth from squalor to the glory of spiritual fulfilment. I knew that the way to God was not by individual self-development and self-realisation but by self-sacrifice for the sake of the world and its resurrection from the dead. Once again Christ was all in all, but He was often made clearer in the breadth of Eastern thought than in the arid dogmatism of much Christian theology, which had all too often erred in the direction of intellectual deduction rather than in direct mystical apprehension and its practical fulfilment.

While my mind was being thus cultivated, I was being initiated into the ministry of healing. Schooled as I was in orthodox allopathic medicine, there was an in-built hostility to any alleged therapy that was not fully tractable to reason. But just as my dereliction had led me to unusual paths of psychological speculation, so my increasing humility made me more receptive to eccentric approaches to healing. It was through the agency of a very fine psychic healer that I was first induced to quit the role of interested observer and start practising the laying-on of hands myself. This healer had the most powerfully developed psychic gifts that I had ever witnessed, but, in addition, he was deeply spiritual in his concern for others. He was a fine teacher, and many people I knew owed much to him. He had little respect for the medical profession and none at all for the Church, at whose hands he had received many rebuffs. There is a tendency amongst certain highly bigoted religionists to attribute all healing gifts that do not fall within the range of religious orthodoxy to demonic influence. While I would agree that certain highly unpleasant people do have remarkable psychic gifts, including the one of contact healing, it is arrogant and unjust to dismiss all psychic healers as evil. Jesus Himself was accused by the religionists of His day of casting out devils by the power of the devil (Mark 3:22-27). His answer, that the devil does not destroy his own works, is worth remembering. Anyone who has even a superficial healing gift is at least potentially on the side of God. But assuredly there is more to healing than the mere amelioration of a bodily malady. If the healer tries to influence others selfishly, his gift can indeed assume a demonic form. But if he leads them towards self-understanding and service for others, he is certainly an agent of light, whatever his religious beliefs. Jesus Himself warned us about people who say "Lord, Lord" but do not act according to God's will. They will not be recognised even if they do remarkable things using the name of Christ (Matthew 7:21-23). What matters is the love and compassion they have to those in need. "In as much as you have done it unto one of the least of these my brethren, ye have done it unto me" (Matthew 25:40).

The memory of my first reaction to practising contact healing still amuses me. I felt as if I were behaving unprofessionally, and I told only a few people about it. To assure myself that I was not really a charlatan, I resolved never to charge anything for my service, a resolve I have mercifully been able to fulfil to this day. It is certainly better not to charge for any spiritual gift, but rather to have some additional employment to supply the means for existence.

I hired a small suite in a poor state of repair, and put my whole body into painting and renovating it — a remarkable achievement for me! At last it was ready for use, and the first patient arrived. I soon learnt that my real gift was the forging of a rapid, close relationship with the person who came to see me. The laying-on of hands was used, if at all, only as the culmination of the interview, and I always followed it by a brief period of silent prayer. On more than one occasion a bodily improvement occurred that caused me to raise my medical eyebrows, but I knew enough about the vagaries of the natural course of chronic diseases not to become over-enthusiastic about this. This was doubly fortunate, for I never looked for results to maintain my faith, and at the same time I saw healing in a far greater context than the mere restoration of bodily health. I began to see the salvation that plays such an important role in the Judeo-Christian tradition as the healing of the whole personality under the guidance of the Spirit of God, who resurrects the soul, mind, and body of the person, and is indeed the integrating centre of the whole personality.

My healing ministry expanded into counselling and spiritual direction, with the laying-on of hands as a sacramental act of dedication. The ministry of healing is man's noblest work of collaboration with God: it includes scientific medicine, psychological understanding, the healing gifts of the Spirit, and the sacraments of the Church. All are God given, and none is pre-eminent over the others. I was later to include the deliverance of deceased personalities who were obsessing those of the living as an occasional part of my healing ministry.

Meanwhile I was studying the works of C. G. Jung in depth, and to these I added the insights of contemporary existential and humanistic psychologists. The writings of Abraham Maslow, Viktor Frankl, and Roberto Assagioli were of great importance. Of the psycho-analytic school Jung was pre-eminent in stressing the reality of the spiritual side of man's conscious life. Frankl, an Austrian Jew who had spent three years in Auschwitz, Dachau, and two other German concentration camps and had had time to meditate on the meaning of his life which seemed to be miraculously preserved in the face of the carnage around him, introduced into psychology the importance of meaning as the basis of fulfilled living. He called his system "Logotherapy." Maslow recognised the spiritual dimension as the final flowering of the full personality of man in the process he called "self-actualisation". The most important of all to me was the still little-known Italian psychiatrist Assagioli, who used meditation in psychotherapy and who understood the importance of the will as no other psychologist had previously done. He had a profound knowledge of Eastern religion, and incorporated Raja Yoga techniques into his system, which he called "Psychosynthesis".

Through the beautiful writings of Martin Buber I began to make contact once more with Judaism, and especially the eighteenth-century mystical movement Hasidism. Great spirituality was, as it were, on my very doorstep, and I had overlooked it in my remote searches. To be sure, I could never return to the restricted, enclosed atmosphere of traditional Judaism, but I did begin to grasp the essential truth of the Jewish insight into God the creator of all things, that when He created them, He saw that they were good. It is this joyous affirmation of life that has not only preserved the Jews despite indescribably terrible suffering, but has given them an influence in the world out of all proportion to their numerical strength. Well was it said that salvation comes of the Jews (John 4:22). The life of Jesus is both the culmination of the Jewish insight into God and its universalisation to all men. The whole meaning of creation, redemption, and sanctification is reflected in His life, through which all creation returns as redeemed free agents sanctified by His Spirit to the Father.

My addresses on spiritual and psychological topics were by this time becoming increasingly well received. At first I spoke to lay groups interested in esoteric teachings, but soon I found myself more and more in clerical company. I found a strong point of contact with members of Anglican religious communities, and I started to give lectures in churches. I could see well enough how the Holy Spirit was moving me inexorably towards a full Christian commitment despite my suspicion of organised religion. I was nevertheless delighted that I, and especially the teaching that came from me, were fully acceptable to many mainstream Christians. It proved the great liberalisation of thought that the Church had undergone since the days of my childhood and adolescence. My theme was the abundance of life — both on earth and in eternity — that a full understanding of Christ can give man. However much I tried to be detached in my psychological thinking, I could never remain long without mentioning Christ, in Whom the fullness of the Godhead dwelt bodily, as a presage of the day when the remainder of mankind would also partake fully of the divine nature that was at present lying dormant within it. This joyous theme filled me with spiritual radiance as I proclaimed it, and my audience responded encouragingly. It was not long before I was invited to conduct retreats, a form of spiritual communication I particularly value, as the group remains entire for at least two days before the members disperse once more. During this time both teaching and communion can really begin to penetrate into the depths of the retreatants' minds.

It was evident that the Holy Spirit was impelling me to active church membership. At the same time I began to see the Church in a more sympathetic light. It was becoming more receptive to ideas that previously would have been regarded with the deepest suspicion, and in its breadth it had a place even for my insights. On the other hand, my own earlier uncritical sympathy for radical views in politics and religion, which I had re-echoed almost automatically in my younger days, began to wane. While I could never be a reactionary, I began to see the full effect of atheistic thinking in even stable, democratic societies. Man swings all too easily from a dogmatic puritanical type of religion to a spineless type of liberalism which culminates in destructive anarchy. The first is the death of all real religious freedom — the freedom conferred by the Holy Spirit — while the second leads to social and moral corruption, which in turn invokes the power of dictatorship to curb it. It is evident that a religious tradition should side neither with the conservative nor the radical elements of society, but should seek to use the insights of both for the proper growth of man and the glory of God. Far from opting out of politics and social conflicts, the truly spiritual man should be deeply involved in them in order to ennoble his particular political party and bring it into the realm of divine order.

I saw the Church, despite its spiritual failings and its past episodes of persecution, cruelty, obscurantism, and fanaticism, as the ultimate bulwark against barbarism. Once God and the transcendent are eliminated from man's range of thought, and man himself becomes the measure of all things, aspiration fails, and people become mere chattels in the hands of their more unscrupulous fellows. The Church is the repository of divine revelation; even if it has often betrayed its custodianship, it has always been sustained by the blessed company of saints and martyrs. If anything that I taught was to be of permanent value — remembering that I spoke not of myself but from the Holy Spirit who inspired me — it would be held and received best by an institution that had the elements of spirituality within it, even if its members did not frequently avail themselves of them.

I also saw that the constant carping criticism of the Church for its various failings — spiritual, intellectual, and social — was unhelpful of change. How much finer it would be to join and help from within rather than to criticise from outside where one was both impregnable and useless! In fact, one only gains through giving of oneself. The motivation for becoming a church member must be love, not the desire to get something for oneself. In the past many people were regular church-goers because they had little else to do with the rather dreary Sundays of those times. The sermon was as much an object of entertainment as the word of the Holy Spirit, while the ritual of the church had theatrical overtones. Nowadays radio and television are the mass media of entertainment, and worship must indeed be in spirit and in truth. Furthermore, the social approbation that accompanied church-going is now a thing of the past. Those who are really "with it" have little use for God — except in a crisis, when they cease to be "with it" and become humble mortals once more! The result of all this has not been a weakening of religious witness so much as a winnowing out of the chaff from the wheat. But if the wheat is to be cultivated and yield a good harvest, it must be fed on spiritual truth and not empty ritual and words. This is the challenge that confronts the Church. I felt that I, at least, could make my contribution to it.

As regards worship, I was happy in all the main denominations. I valued the beauty of the Catholic liturgy and also the

Protestant insight into the priesthood of all believers. In the end my choice lay between the Church of England and the Religious Society of Friends. The Quakers, though small in number, were the only group whose witness seemed to me to have been consistently Christian. Their opposition to slavery, injustice, and war was absolute, their honesty profound, and their form of silent contemplative worship corresponded exactly with my own concept of prayer. But in the end I felt that a broader, more comprehensive, more sacramental tradition would be the right one for my particular gifts, and so I became an Anglican. As usual I entered into this new commitment with fear and trepidation, for I was afraid of sacrificing my spiritual freedom and enclosing myself in a narrow credal type of religion. I was to learn that by entering a major denomination of broad sympathies I was finding a real home in a discipline that bore the imprint of Catholic spirituality tested over the centuries, while at the same time enjoying the freedom of private judgment germane to the Protestant tradition. Allowing for the inadequacy of any credal statement to do justice to the supreme majesty of God, I found that the two basic creeds of the Church, when interpreted mystically, gave as good an account of the nature and action of Christ as could be put into intellectual formulation. Such an explicit creed can be less burdensome than the implicit beliefs of many spiritual groups and societies who pride themselves on their complete freedom from dogma. In fact, no one could happily remain within the proximity of such a group who did not subscribe to its general attitude. In other words, all spiritual groups and societies are bound by a common dogma, and those that formulate this directly often have a greater freedom of action than those who do not face the issue except by indirect emotional pressure.

I found I had to surrender or modify none of my previous metaphysical views; on the contrary, these were often strengthened and confirmed by my deeper understanding of the Bible and by the teachings of the Fathers of the Church. At the same time I gathered great support from the fellowship of many fine people, who, even if they could not follow me in deeper speculation, at least were in unity with me over the important issues confronting the world. The sacraments of the Church were a source of spiritual renewal, and the great peace I derived from the Eucharist widened my understanding of communal prayer. But the most noteworthy result of my total commitment to Christ was a deepening of my spiritual life. This manifested itself outwardly by augmented spiritual gifts of speaking and healing and inwardly by greater composure and joy in everyday life and an increased intensity of prayer.

So my life has progressed. The professional side has flourished mightily; in ordinary circumstances its activities — teaching, writing, and hospital work — would have been sufficient to occupy my time. But it is balanced almost exactly by the "spiritual" side (as if any work done with devotion is not spiritual), which embraces the ministry of healing, delivering many addresses to diverse groups of people, conducting retreats, and giving instruction about meditation and prayer. At one time I dreaded being asked how I spent my spare time; now I am no longer embarrassed, for I have none. Yet I am not fatigued, and my health, praise be to God, has remained excellent. Over the past eighteen years I have had occasion to spend only four days away from work on account of illness.

All truly spiritual activities are forms of recreation to me, and the inner peace that comes through the practice of meditation and prayer is a very real way of resting while working. I did have one valuable hobby, piano playing, but this was willingly sacrificed when I entered the healing ministry; the unavailability of time made this sad decision inevitable. But its fruits are permanent: a real understanding and enjoyment of a vast range of music that would have been impossible without practical knowledge of an instrument. Art has always inspired me to a deeper knowledge of God, and no form of art is more eloquent and evocative than music.

When I consider, from the vantage point of middle age, how my life has unfolded, I am full of gratitude and wonder. It has indeed been precarious living. But everything I have attained has been given to me through silent listening and waiting. Whenever I have asserted myself, I have failed to achieve what

I desired and have become desperately unhappy. The prodiga-
lity of God's goodness to me is a source of great thanksgiving.

But from him to whom much is given, much is expected.
This candid autobiographical account is a payment of part of
the debt I owe. It is no small thing to expose oneself to the gaze
of an indifferent, if not hostile reader in the hope that the path
to life trodden by one particular aspirant may be of help to
others also on the way.

Let it not be thought that the course has been completed.
The summons to full service is only now being decisively
obeyed.

II
The Language of the Path

1

The Glory of a Person

THE NOMENCLATURE OF man's spiritual anatomy is intricate and controversial. It is important nevertheless to make some attempt at definition in order to clarify our concepts of personal identity. At one extreme there is the behaviouristic psychologist who accepts only the physical body governed by the brain; he does not recognise mind as anything apart from the response of the brain to various stimuli and the conditioning it has undergone through experiences in the past. At the other extreme there is the theosophical view of personality, itself largely derived from Hindu metaphysics, that not only distinguishes non-material mind from the physical body through which it manifests itself during life on this earth, but also grades the mind into various hierarchies of perception up to the supreme awareness of ultimate reality. While I would not dismiss this view, and indeed find it fascinating to meditate upon, I have not been particularly helped by it in my own understanding of spiritual experience. It is a complex scheme which at the most is merely a final refinement.

The Aspects of Personality

Personally I respond to the Platonic concept of human nature with its tripartite division of "body", "soul", and "spirit". This still seems to me to be the most helpful approach in defining personality. As such it was used to masterly effect by St. Paul who was, amongst other qualities, a brilliant spiritual psychologist, as his letter to the Romans especially demonstrates. I would add the "mind" to this list, and define soul as its most exalted manifestation. The mind is the mental, behavioural component that feels emotionally, thinks rationally, and wills consciously (at least in properly integrated people). It is a matter of fundamental importance whether this essential part of human experience can be attributed entirely to the activity of the brain, for if this is indeed the case, as the behaviouristic psychologist would assert, it puts out of court any permanent aspect of personality such as might survive the death of the body. It also effectively demolishes any personal will that is independent of previous conditioning. The question is still an open one with most professional workers rejecting the dualism of mind and body, since this denial accords well with the current atheistic positivism dominant in many academic circles. But those who have thought more deeply about the matter are less sure. The finer nuances of personality that express themselves in ethical behaviour, aesthetic appreciation, and self-giving sacrifice in love do not fall easily into the range of mere behavioural responses to stimuli. It may yet be that the mind is separate from the body yet functioning in intimate connexion with it through the agency of the brain. The data of psychical research, against which there is great emotionally based opposition amongst many academicians, suggest strongly that a focus of consciousness may function at a distance from the body of a psychically sensitive person. My own inner experiences have confirmed a dualistic view of mind and body, but it must be stressed that the personality is a unified whole with the parts working in one accord.

In this connexion, the Christian doctrine of the Holy Trinity is a cosmic application of a similar unity in multiplicity, and as such is particularly valuable in envisaging the action of the one eternal Godhead in the world of form.

Properties of Mind

The fundamental quality of mind, however we conceive it, is its tendency to react to outer circumstances in the environment and inner sensations arising from the physical body that is associated with it. This response is the basis of consciousness, which reveals itself in feeling, thinking, and willing a deliberate action. To some people the word "mind" is synonymous with the thinking, or intellectual function, but it is preferable to extend it to embrace all aspects of consciousness manifesting themselves in volition, thought, and feeling. The other word that can be used in the same context is "psyche", which is sometimes equated with the soul, but whose application should preferably be extended to include all aspects of personal consciousness.

The Personal Self

The central focus of the conscious mind is the "personal self", or "existential self." It is the awareness we have of our own identity, but paradoxically it is hidden from most people. It makes itself felt most keenly during periods of crisis when choices are open to us and decisions have to be made. I speak heree of decisions of a moral nature when the choices open, whatever they may be, are unpleasant but inescapable. The type of decision that brings the personal self into finest focus is one in which we have to choose between doing what we know in our deepest awareness is morally wrong but expedient in terms of the approval of those around us, and what is clearly morally right but in opposition to the general feeling of the society in which we live. The personal self can also be experienced during meditation when we have ceased to identify with our body, our emotions, and our thoughts, and are quiet within ourselves. The reason why we, as thoughtless individuals, are seldom aware of our inner identity is because we are all too often moved hither and thither by outside circumstances and inner drives and impulses that arise from bodily desires and the memories of past events that bear a strong emotional charge. The personal self can be identified with the "ego" of Freudian psychology, provided this is not seen simply as a flitting centre of consciousness by which we know ourselves at each moment of time, when it would be merely that identification we develop with an outer circumstance or inner drive that is dominating us at a particular moment.

The Unconscious

The range of the mind is much greater than merely the

conscious self. This is, as it were, encompassed by a "field of consciousness" of which we are immediately aware: it consists of an incessant flow of ideas, impulses, thoughts, and feeling which we can observe and judge in detachment. This has been called the "mind-stream" by William James, and, as I have already observed, can easily be mistaken for the personal self by those who are not in command of themselves.

But much of the contents of the mind are not within the field of immediate consciousness at all, and this is called the "unconscious". Some of the contents of the unconscious resemble that of the field of consciousness and are under easy recall by the memory. But by far the greater part of the unconscious consists of psychic elements that are so powerfully submerged, or repressed, that they are hidden persistently from the field of consciousness. This realm of the mind is the place of action of the psycho-analyst, for in it are stored the primitive urges and basic drives of survival, sex, and self-assertiveness that are part of our animal inheritance, as well as painful personal memories too unpleasant to be confronted in full consciousness. But these elements are not completely latent, for they tend to be released during sleep when they may be brought to full awareness, usually in the form of symbols, as vivid dreams. It is evident that this part of the unconscious is related to our animal nature and the darker personal experiences we have undergone in the past. It can, in terms of values, be called the "lower unconscious".

In this valuation the "lower unconscious" can be contrasted with the "higher unconscious", or the "superconscious." This too is unconscious, inasmuch as its contents are normally beyond easy recall to the field of consciousness, but its nature is high and spiritual inasmuch as its drives are exalted and ennobling. They tend in their action to fulfil the realisation of our full humanity, and encompass humanitarian, ethical, altruistic, and even heroic actions and ideals, and they include aesthetic performance and self-sacrifice for other people. There is a tendency to explain away these exalted impulses as mere sublimations of elements of the lower unconscious which have been thwarted: religious actions could be an outlet for a failed self-assertion in power or sex, and altruism a way of dealing with the frustrated will to power over other people. But superconscious impulses are as spontaneous and unexpected as those of the lower unconscious, and they break into the field of consciousness suddenly in the form of intuition, inspiration, illumination, creative imagination, and universal love. The sudden scientific discovery is often due to a superconscious inspiration, and it is not surprising that geniuses are most in contact with this area of the mind. In most geniuses it would seem that one particular superconscious impulse (such as artistic creativity, scientific research, or mathematical understanding) impinges on their field of consciousness, whereas the great universal geniuses who are gifted in many fields, appear to have their field of consciousness in permanent communication with the superconscious part of the mind.

It should be noted here that while the Freudian "id" can be equated with the lower unconscious in terms of animal and purely personal contents, the Freudian "super-ego" is different from the contents of the superconscious. The super-ego arises from the conditioning that the developing child undergoes at the hands of its parents and the society in which it lives and is educated. The values of that society are impressed on the growing person as the end of proper behaviour and living, and he then accepts them, albeit unconsciously, as the ideal for his own life. In this way he may be crippled psychologically, and prevented from realising his own real identity. The "super-ego" is an imposed dictatorship from sources outside oneself that dominate one's attitudes to life and interfere with one's own judgment. Of course, we cannot learn the ways of worldly life except by conditioning from those more experienced in those ways than we are as little children. This is the basis of education, but if our own identity is completely overshadowed by outer conditioning, we can never grow into full people. At this stage the super-ego becomes a destructive force in our lives.

Likewise the lower unconscious is not in itself evil. Without its drives we would neither survive nor procreate. But it becomes demonic when it is dominant in our personalities, for its drives are selfish and enclosed. St. Paul in the seventh chapter of his letter to the Romans contrasts the law of the flesh and its tendency to destruction with the law of the spirit which is life-giving. Even when there is an earnest desire to live nobly according to the spirit, the selfish law of the flesh finally wins. If only the spirit could triumph over the flesh, not so as to diminish it, but to resurrect it from corruptibility to everlasting life! It is the balance between the "lower" and "higher" aspects of the unconscious that is to be sought. A domination of the lower leads to selfish gratification and eventual death; a domination of the higher leads to an impractical other-worldliness that prevents the proper functioning of the physical body. St. Paul rightly sees that the power of Christ alone can ensure spiritual life and bodily resurrection.

The Spiritual Self and the Soul

If the painful process of knowing ourselves, as enjoined on us all by the Delphic oracle, is pursued, we find that we are not simply the outer appurtenances that we show to the world: age, sex, race, profession, and social class. Nor are we the emotional responses or ideas that assail us continually: these vary in intensity and are evanescent, and cannot be equated with a permanent focus of identity. It is when we have discovered the personal self within us, usually at the height of a moral crisis, that we are beginning to establish our unique identity. At the same time unconscious depths are revealed in us during dreams or when we react perversely in sudden unexpected situations. The technique of psycho-analysis helps to define elements, or "complexes", in the unconscious that are interfering with our inner knowledge of our own identity. These are comparable to moving clouds that obliterate the sun's rays, the sun being the true self of the person, which is normally deeply placed in the superconscious. There are moments given by grace, when a greater reality of our being is revealed to us. In these blessed periods, the personal self, with its enclosed isolation, lonely and fighting for its preservation, seems to open out and becomes luminous, extensive, loving, all-embracing and yet free. From the grim separateness of personal selfhood, there is a participation of an intimate communion with all other selves. And yet the identity of the person is not only unchallenged;

it is clearer and more complete than ever. This is the experience of the "true", "spiritual", or "higher self", and it is the essence of the "soul" of the person. Nowadays it is also often called the "transpersonal self". The experience of the radiant, all-pervading spiritual self is the path of mysticism: the aim of the mystic journey is the discovery of one's true self, and gaining an understanding of its relationship with the cosmos and with God.

But in fact there is only one self; the personal self, or ego, that we are aware of when we come to ourselves in a crisis or during meditation is the dull reflection of the superconscious spiritual self in the tarnished mirror of our conditioned personality and in the world around us. If we lived in the abundance that Christ spoke of and witnessed to in His life, the personal self would glow in spiritual radiance as does the spiritual self, and indeed the two selves would coincide. In the unitive life, the ultimate state of mysticism, the mystic lives perpetually at the level of the spiritual self.

The soul of a person is that quality that proclaims his uniqueness, and shows itself primarily in terms of value judgments. It is seen most radiantly in the form of the spiritual self, but its influence is far from absent in the more earthy personal self. The quality of soul penetrates the lower reaches of the mind, and brings with it a regeneration of the body. It permeates the whole personality in the mature person. The soul is paradoxically not only the unique quality of every man, but is also shared and reaches its fullest development in giving of itself absolutely in love to others.

The Spirit

The main qualities of the soul, which is the most exalted manifestation of the mind, or psyche, are creative imagination, intuitive understanding, and spiritual realisation. This last is a direct illuminative apprehension of the nature and destination of the journey that the soul has to undergo for its own completion. According to the teachings of the mystics there is an aspect of the soul which they call "the spark", "the centre of the soul", or "the apex of the soul" which is the highest and holiest part of the spiritual self. It is called the "spirit" (St.

Paul speaks of "pneuma"), and by it, or in it, the reality of God, however we perceive Him (whether personally as in Western theistic religion, or transpersonally as in Eastern mystical religion), is known. The mystic would affirm that God is immanent in the Spirit. The Quakers speak of "that of God in every man". Other more theologically orientated religionists who see God only in a transcendent category would describe the spirit as the organ whereby the soul can attain a knowledge of God. Personally I favour the first view, that God is present in His immanent mode in all creation, and especially self-conscious mankind. It is by this fact that we may become partakers of the divine nature (2 Peter 1:4), when we are really spirit-infused persons.

The spirit of man is the candle of the Lord (Proverbs 20:27). It is that which dares us to develop into full persons. In undeveloped men this power of the spirit that comes through God's Holy Spirit (the lord and giver of life) is used selfishly and destructively through a perverted will. But as a person comes more under the domination of the spiritual self, or soul, so the spirit in him shines more brightly and leads him on to spiritual realisation. Then he lives more for others and less for himself alone; eventually the great injunction to love one's neighbour as oneself becomes possible. It does not mean self-denial so much as a real concern for all people, including oneself, all of whom are seen to be made in the image of God.

The Person

A person is an individual in whom body, mind, and soul are integrated into a working whole under the guidance of the spirit. The concept of a person is a very high one, and there are few of us who are real persons. To be a person does not require great intellectual understanding, or psychic magnetism, or physical strength, or social eligibility. It requires only the integrity to be oneself, which in turn requires one to know oneself. Our life on earth is one of fashioning the body and mind that our parents have bequeathed to us into a unified organism under the control of the soul, or spiritual self, which in all probability is not inherited but has had experience of a previous existence. The integrating centre is the spirit, through which the Holy Spirit performs His sanctifying work.

A person is not perfect, just as the soul itself is not perfect. Its experience in the limitation of a physical body and the lower unconscious is one of chastening and suffering. It is the spirit alone that is perfect, for it is our inner image of God. But most of us are a very great distance from a knowledge of the spirit, and are therefore incomplete persons.

The incarnate Christ is our measure of a complete person; in Him in truth does the Godhead shine as uncreated light through an organism that transmits that light unsullied and undimmed. St. Paul sees this state of full humanity as one of coming to the unity inherent in our faith and of our knowledge of Christ, so that we attain to full manhood measured by nothing less than the full stature of Christ (Ephesians 4:13).

If we see a person in this light, the Persons of the Holy Trinity become clearer. They are not merely attributes of God but full representatives of the ineffable Godhead in the world of becoming.

2

Free Will and Spiritual Aspiration

THE FUNCTION OF will, at least in a context of free choice, is a perennial problem of philosophy. Are we really free to choose or is our way predetermined? The view of religious culture is that man has free will to choose his way of life and discern his own spiritual path. But many philosophers deny this freedom. The behaviouristically orientated psychologist, who sees all action as arising from the brain's response to stimuli, and behaviour as a response to past conditioning of the brain to various stimuli, would take the extreme view against the concept of free will. And it must be acknowledged that behaviouristic psychology has shed important light on modes of human behaviour. But there is more to human experience than can be accommodated in the view of pure behaviourism. The nuances of altruistic love, self-sacrifice, and personal integrity in the face of public hostility speak of a higher mode of mental activity than a merely predictable response of the brain to a pleasant stimulus.

The Enslaved Will

The will, in its broadest context, can be thought of as the active response of the person to a tangible desire. Each desire drives the person on towards its own satisfaction, but the active response incurred in this transaction cannot be described as free without considerable qualification. A person's whole life may, for instance, be devoted to making money or achieving some position of power within the community in which he lives. The will of such a person may appear to be immensely strong and well focussed, and yet it may be enslaved to a desire deeply placed in the unconscious. How many very powerful men, tyrants to those immediately subservient to them, like their family, and a source of admiration and envy to those further off, are really the slaves to a deep inner sense of inferiority, possibly social or intellectual! They have been driven on a course of self-assertion to assuage the unconscious desire for recognition and security. And behind this façade of ruthless power over others, there lies a frightened child, longing desperately to be acknowledged and loved for himself alone. In due course this façade may crumble, perhaps through outside failure or inner physical and mental collapse, and the little child is then revealed in his pristine helplessness. Such a person has never been free while he was asserting himself, but only begins to know the meaning of freedom once all his pretensions have been crushed. Much of our impassioned outer self-expression has little to do with free will; it arises either from unconscious drives within us, or from the conditioning we have acquired from the environment in which we have lived and been educated (an aspect of the Freudian super-ego).

The Conscious Will

We can in this way be propelled by the psychic energy that emanates from unconscious drives. Though apparently active, we are in fact being passively driven by forces outside our own control. No wonder the psycho-analyst has little respect for the concept of free will. Even apparently fine religious works may originate from unresolved feelings of guilt over half-forgotten actions or beliefs in the past, and the energy of our ungratified sexual drives may be sublimated in aesthetic performance. But when we begin to know the personal, or existential self, we also begin to glimpse an aspect of will over which we have a conscious control. It is then that the freedom of the will becomes possible.

As I have already said, the personal self makes itself known when we have to choose between two courses of action on moral grounds. The implied judgment based on values — and over which no authority outside ourselves can give a final verdict — brings the personal self into full focus, and its action is an act of will freed from bondage to forces outside ourselves. This is the heart of the "conscience" that we know deeply placed in ourselves.

Conscience itself is a vague and rather unsatisfactory psychological concept, because it is the resultant of at least three factors: the conditioning impressed on us by our parents and teachers (the super-ego), group loyalty to those around us, and a deeper awareness of our own true nature which is the core of the personal self (through which the spiritual self, or soul, shines radiantly in such a time of moral crisis). When we can detach our inner awareness of the right attitude from that based on our previous conditioning or that demanded by those people amongst whom we work, we are beginning to experience our real identity. And let it be said that the "right" response can be judged only in terms of the personal growth it stimulates and the spiritual understanding that accrues from it. Judgments of right or wrong actions in terms of immediate results are invariably short-sighted. What appears to be a good result may have, later, less pleasant repercussions; what appears to be a disaster may bring with it a later train of good fortune. The Bhagavadgita states the law of action perfectly: "To action alone hast thou a right and never at all to its fruits; let not the fruits of action be thy motive; neither let there be in thee any attachment to inaction" (Chapter 2, verse 47). This disinterestedness towards results is the heart of spiritual action; it is called "holy indifference" in the Christian tradition and has been practised by its saints of all generations. In such an action the person is in control and his will is free of all motives save the burning one of living and working in present perfection.

The Free Will

The action of the personal self is never completely free in the sense that it has absolute licence to satisfy itself. This is because the person does not live in isolation; he is in physical and psychical contact with the world around him and especially with the remainder of mankind. Furthermore, his life is not static; it follows its inevitable course to disease, old age, and death. The law of the lower unconscious, or the flesh as St. Paul puts it, is inexorably one of death. He who is chained to the flesh and its desires is imprisoned in mortality. But the law of the spirit is life eternal, and its drives come to us from the superconscious. The fundamental desire of a fully alive person is one of meaning, an understanding of the nature of the strange process of life and death to which our flesh is heir and of the destiny of the self we know through the crises and choices of existence. This desire for meaning takes us on a path of exploration past the isolated self and its demands for gratification to a concern for the world in which we live and the people around us. It shows us the meaning of love, of sacrifice of our personal self in order to attain a knowledge of the immortal spiritual self which is the source of the personal self. It leads us finally to unitive knowledge of God,, Who reveals Himself to us in the spirit within us.

From this it can be deduced that the will can either be enslaved to the lower drives of the person and devote itself to self-satisfaction even at the expense of others, or it can serve the highest it knows and lead the person on to full humanity, even the humanity that was manifest in the Incarnate Christ. Then the will of the person knows and serves the will of God; "in His will is our peace" (Dante, *Paradiso*, Canto 3, verse 85). Well is it said in the Collect of Peace in the Book of Common Prayer, "O God...whose service is perfect freedom." In the service of God we are freed from the shackles of all mortal things, and enter into a knowledge of the love of God. Instead of being tied to mortal things, including our own bodies, we control and govern them and become agents for their resurrection from the dead to the realm of spiritual reality, which is eternal life.

Free Will and Predestination

The more we consider life in general and look back on our own lives in particular, the more do we come to see how little control we really have in the outer course of our earthly destiny. There is indeed a power far above our understanding that knows about us and what is to become of us. Jesus reminds us that not even a sparrow falls to the ground without God knowing, and even the hairs on our heads have been counted (Matthew 10:29-30). Those who have the psychic gift of precognition, which sometimes manifests itself in dreams, are aware to what extent the future is pre-ordained. But one thing is not ordained, our final response to the unknown future. We can either fail, as Peter in his weakness did after the betrayal of Jesus whom he denied three times, or else we can move to realms of sublime self-sacrificial heroism. And even if we do fail on one occasion, we can be redeemed later on, as was Peter himself.

In my own life it is clear that I was called to active Christian ministry from my earliest days, and this first required suffi-cient spiritual growth to render my service valid. I could, however, quite easily have rejected the call, as Jonah tried to do in that magnificent parable of the Old Testament. But had I acted thus, I would certainly have brought increasing psycholo-gical disturbance on myself which might well have culminated in a fatal physical malady or even in a termination of my life by my own hand. As I learnt from my own experience, the will is most active when it is quiet and receptive, causing the whole personality to wait on God and learn what He wants us to do to be full persons. This is the meaning of prayer. Thus the concepts of free will and predestination, far from opposing each other, are each necessary for the fulfilment of the other. We are predestined to become real persons, made in the image of God, in the fullness of Christ Incarnate. For this to happen our wills have to be freed from all desires other than that for God Himself, in whose service we alone can be free to become as He was when He revealed Himself in the form of a man. The greatest freedom a man can have is to become a real person.

The Use of the Will

Many are called, but few are chosen (Matthew 22:14). The reason for this is that only a small number respond to the call and even fewer have the persistence to remain to the end. The will, once it is acknowledged as the action of the personal self and is manifested in the execution of clear decisions during crises, has then to marshal the psychic energy of the uncon-scious drives so that these become part of the person and no longer separate, dominating forces. In other words, the drives to self-preservation, sexual activity, and self-assertiveness have to be controlled and used constructively. The sexual impulse, for example, when it is in control of the person, can lead him to animal bestiality. On the other hand, sexuality can be a most beautiful human attribute, flowing out in warmth and radiance to other people and drawing them into a greater community of friends, provided it is under the guidance of the personal self, which in turn mirrors the soul of the person.

It is by an act of will that man leaves behind his pre-occupation with the animal drives of the lower unconscious and ventures forth into the superconscious realms of universal love and brotherhood, where self is sacrificed in love for the greater community. In this way talents, once hidden, are now brought to the light of consciousness and developed. The highest aspiration is the will to good, in which one's whole being is dedicated to the divine quest and the transfiguration and resurrection of the world through love. This is very different from mere goodwill, which can so often remain a pious attitude without any driving force behind it to make it real.

The will should be informed and reinforced by the Holy Spirit in the act of prayer. Will that derives from personal desire, no matter how noble it appears on the surface, without the humility of waiting for God's redeeming word, tends inevitably to dictate to others, especially those whom one really wants to help. In other words, personal will is arrogant, tyrannical, and intractable until it is informed of divine grace. This comes to us when we are humble and receptive. At this point the will is no longer assertive in proclaiming the views and desires of the person; it is instead quiet and still in prayer, waiting for God and acting only after hearing the divine command.

The well-known injunction of St. Augustine emphasises this: "Love, and do what you will." The person who really loves is filled with God's love, and is thereby cleansed of personal longings and desires. Only then are his motives pure, and his will is inspired by God Himself. Whatever he does is a blessing to many. And he will persist to the end, for "lo, I am with you alway, even unto the end of the world" (Matthew 28:20).

3

The Psychical and the Spiritual Planes of Reality

THE RANGE OF the mind, or psyche, is vast. The personal self is merely the tip of the iceberg of consciousness, most of which is submerged. The spiritual self, through which the soul radiates most powerfully, penetrates and illuminates the vast range of mind, at least in a "self-actualised person" — by which I mean a person who is well on the way to establishing his true identity, who has passed beyond the conditioning of his surroundings and enslavement to the selfish unconscious drives of self-preservation, sex, and comfort, and is free to be himself and use the talents previously latent in him. In the more average mass of human beings there is little awareness of the fixed centre that we know as the personal self, let alone the radiance of the spiritual self, of which, as I have already stated, the personal self is merely a dull reflection in a tarnished, undeveloped mind.

The Collective Unconscious

The mind is complex in form, and has no fixed limits or boundaries. It is in fellowship with the minds of other people through the means of conscious rational communication that we use in social intercourse, such as speech and writing, and in addition there is a non-rational, unwilled communion between the minds of all sentient beings. This communion is mediated through the "collective unconscious" (described so admirably by Jung), and it extends from the psyche of the earliest members of the human race to the most recent additions.

Through our individual participation in the collective unconscious, we experience symbolic images of high psychic power
that have been in currency since the beginning of man's
history. Many of these symbols have important information to
impart about the state of our unconscious and its degree of
integration with our conscious life. A living integration of
various elements of the unconscious — autonomous complexes,
archetypal images and themes (that have their origin deep in
man's psychic pre-history), and symbols that have the ability to
transform our inner attitudes — with consciousness forms the
process of "individuation" which is the heart of Jung's
psychological theory. As the two are progressively integrated,
so there is a tendency for the true self, both in its personal and
spiritual mode, to be revealed and at last we begin to live as
real persons.

The individual psyche is indeed in intimate communion
with the psyche of the world and its creatures. Well did
Heraclitus say, "You can never find out the boundaries of the
soul, so deep are they." The boundaries of the psyche are not
only immeasurably deep but they are also inextricably woven
with the soul of the whole created universe. It is in this respect
that we are members one of another (Ephesians 4:25), and if we
were living fully in the Spirit, this membership would be
realised in our conscious lives also. But then our present world
of separation and death would pass away and Christ would be
all and in all (Colossians 3:11).

Extrasensory Communication

Since there is a communication between the individual mind
and the total psychic history of mankind (to say nothing of the
minds of those people closely associated with us either by
blood relationship or community of interests), it is to be
expected that we are from time to time subject to flashes of
information that come directly to us without the mediation of
such rational sensory perception as speech that is heard or
writing that is seen. Indeed, it is surprising that such "extrasensory perception", or psychic communication, is not of more

frequent occurrence than it appears to be. The distinguished French philosopher Henri Bergson, himself a student of psychical research and in his day a president of the Society for Psychical Research, put forward the hypothesis that extrasensory perception is the normal mode of communication between minds, but that the brain acts as a censor to prevent the influx into consciousness of undifferentiated psychic information, which though of great theoretical interest is of no practical use to us in the everyday running of our lives. I agree with Bergson. The most primitive races seem to have the greatest psychic rapport not only with each other as people but also with their natural environment. On the other hand, their intellectual ability is modest, and their awareness of self-identity rudimentary. This state of psychic rapport has idyllic overtones, but such people are geared to a low level of human performance and are not easily adaptable to outside circumstances of interference or disaster.

As man grows in intelligence, so the rational faculty of the mind dominates, and with it he sees himself apart from the realm of nature and ultimately isolated even from his fellows. The natural tendency to strive selfishly for self-preservation at the expense of others, which, if carried out logically to the end, would lead to war, destruction, and the total annihilation of the human race (and perhaps the entire planet now that man is equipped with nuclear energy) is fortunately offset by the innate nobility that is also part of human nature, residing, as we have already seen, in the "higher" part of the unconscious. The more isolated man is, the less amenable he is to extrasensory perception; indeed, the experience of the personal self at the moment of conscious decision in a crisis is an experience also of total isolation from the greater community who previously tended to carry the person along with it. But as one proceeds onwards, guided by the drives that come from the superconscious and manifesting themselves in value judgments which lead one on to full humanity, so the domination of the rationality of the personal self loosens, and the reason becomes subject to higher intuitions emanating from the superconscious and especially from the spiritual self. At this stage of "self-actualisation", extrasensory perception again plays its part in leading the person to full inner development. But now the source of information is no longer crudely psychic; it is increasingly spiritual. This is not to say that the "higher", more spiritual ranges of extrasensory information are not also psychically conveyed, but that they are no longer concerned with the person as an isolated unit, and instead with his corporate membership in the body of mankind, whose centre is God.

In this respect we see the difference between the psychical and the spiritual planes of reality; the psychical planes are personal in scope, speaking directly to the isolated individual and tending to exalt him; the spiritual planes are transpersonal, inspiring the person to move beyond personal isolation to that self-giving which is the prerequisite of union with God.

Planes of Psychical Communication

It seems that psychical communication reaches all realms of the individual psyche, from the depths of the lower unconscious with its submerged blackness of unrealised personal desire that can all too easily assume a demonic character, to the heights of the superconscious with its noble aspirations culminating in the vision of God enthroned in the holiest part of the spiritual self, which as I have said, is called the "apex," "centre" or "spark" of the soul, or simply the "spirit". If a person is frustrated through the failure of his conscious life and the repression of deep inner drives of self-assertion, there may be an irruption of unconscious psychic energy into his field of consciousness, and this may lead to destructive, criminal actions. Unless this "shadow" side, present in all of us, is fully accepted and redeemed, it is liable to invade in a demonic form and acquire an identity of its own. It can influence other weak, susceptible people, themselves frustrated and emotionally unbalanced, not only by way of conscious communication in speech and writing, but also by extrasensory contact. In this way a general black mood can spread rapidly throughout an entire community, and precipitate demonic behaviour. The advent of Nazism and its effect on possibly the most civilised nation in the world is a terrible example of the power of demonic psychic communication on a sensitive, frustrated population.

If such dark personalities survive physical death, and I have no doubt that they do, it is quite possible that they could obsess, or even actively possess, the personalities of weak people still alive in the flesh. The prerequisites for this type of obsession are a weak, unbalanced personality and a tendency towards psychic sensitivity such as is encountered in mediumistic types of people. If such a person were to dabble with the occult, the danger of psychic invasion would be a real one. This type of psychical communication is of the lowest order; it impinges on the lower unconscious with its drives towards personal satisfaction without a higher concern for the well-being of other people. The psychism of primitive races is usually, but not always, of this type, and some types of occultism also tap this dark psychic reservoir.

Another, far less undesirable type of psychical communication impinges on the conscious personal self, which itself is a dull reflection of the soul. This type of communication usually takes the form of a strong mental impression that appears to come spontaneously to the person, invading his train of thought and disturbing it peremptorily. It gives him information from some other mind, either still associated with a physical body or else in an immaterial form beyond the grave, and this information is subsequently substantiated and confirmed. This modality of extrasensory communication between two minds is called "telepathy". Sometimes the information is of a more emotional nature. Sometimes it is transformed into words or visions by the psyche of the sensitive recipient (this is called "clairaudience" or "clairvoyance" respectively). On some occasions a clairvoyant person may "see" (with the inner eye of the soul) an event taking place a great distance away.

Another remarkable psychic faculty is the sudden perception of events destined to occur in the future; this is called "precognition", and sometimes it manifests itself in visual configuration. The reverse aspect is "retrocognition", in which the psyche may be attuned to the past history of a person or a locality; this, in minor degrees, is a not uncommon gift, for many people can sense "atmospheres" where there have been conflict or evil doings in the past, or alternatively the hallowed peace of a country church made valid by the prayers of past generations of humble believers.

Of an even higher plane of psychical communication are the teachings that come through some "mediums," or "sensitives" as they are preferably called. These teachings have superconscious overtones, and tend to lead the person away from selfishness to a more active concern with abiding spiritual values. It is probable that many of these communications really arise in the minds of the sensitives themselves, and are therefore psychologically induced rather than psychically transmitted, but a few of the higher teachings do bear the impress of an advanced mind in a realm beyond human knowledge. Nevertheless, I would hesitate to apply the term "spiritual" to even the highest communications of this type, no matter how edifying their content, for they come to the personal self, and tend to confirm the strength of the self rather than lead it to the vision of God. True saintliness does not follow psychical communication from even the most advanced sources, whether on earth or in the life of the world to come. At most, these sources afford one knowledge of things, processes, and techniques. But they cannot provide the only knowledge that ultimately counts for anything at all, the unitive knowledge of God. Each of the great higher religions of the world has its complement of saints, who have trodden the spiritual path that leads to God Himself. But occultism, in the framework that I have already described, leads at best only to enhanced personal power and greater knowledge of the universe. No wonder experienced spiritual directors of all the major religious traditions advise their aspirants to acknowledge psychical phenomena without becoming trapped in their glamour, and to aspire only to the unitive knowledge of God.

Spiritual Communication

The highest of all psychical communication comes from God by way of the spirit to the spiritual self, or soul. It transcends personal isolation, and leads the aspirant from the isolation of the personal self to the full participation in the world of eternal reality. It is in this context that the famous words of Jesus ring true: "Whosoever will come after me, let him deny himself, and take up his cross, and follow me. For whosoever will save his life shall lose it, but whosoever shall lose his life for my sake and the gospel's, the same shall save it" (Mark 8:34-35). In the context of this quotation the Greek word "psyche" is used to denote life; it can also be used in the sense of soul or person, as in the words that immediately follow the above quotation: "What shall it profit a man, if he shall gain the whole world at the cost of his true self (or soul)" (Mark 8:36)? To arrive at the unitive knowledge of God we have to be prepared to sacrifice our very selves (or our very lives), to walk on a hidden path of self-giving in faith. We have to be bereft of personal self-seeking in order to find the spiritual self that is the source of all personality. When we are as little children once more, God can reveal Himself to us as transpersonal love, uncreated light, and fulfilling purpose. We in turn cease to be finite individuals and become complete persons; our identity finds its validity not in isolation but in intimate participation with the whole creation. Being no longer finite entities, we become persons in the universal body, even the full body of Christ seen in His cosmic form. This is the heart of mystical illumination; in it one escapes from limited selfhood and enters into full personality.

I have described my own experience of illumination in the autobiographical section of this book. To compare it with even the highest occult teaching, such as might be transmitted psychically from a source of wisdom beyond the grave, is like comparing eternal life with an alleged communication from a friend who has passed beyond the death of the physical body. Spiritual reality is the culmination of self-knowledge; it implies the swallowing up of the personal self into the spiritual self. When we live in the form of the spiritual self, we are real persons even as Christ was in the human mode. But He lived in the form of the spirit also, for in Him divinity and humanity co-inhere. In Him soul is infused perfectly with the spirit within it. "The first man Adam was made a living soul (psyche); the last Adam was made a quickening spirit (pneuma)" (1 Corinthians 15:45). In us we can, at our present state of being, hope only that the soul may infuse the remainder of the psyche and the body; a knowledge of the spirit is still hidden from us. The important exception is that of the mystics of the human race, who gain glimpses of it.

The Heart of Spirituality

Although truly spiritual communication is a thing apart — and may be called "supernatural" inasmuch as it originates beyond the natural order from the ineffable Godhead Itself — it can, and indeed does, interpenetrate all other modes of communication that impinge on the psyche. The very distinction between spiritual and material, or sacred and secular, is ultimately invalid, for the spiritual mode finds its place in all actions, whether physical or psychical, that lead us to a fuller knowledge of God. Whatever leads us to a knowledge of God is spiritually based; it also leads us away from preoccupation with ourselves to a fuller participation in the world's affairs and the concerns of other people. All this is summarised by Jesus' two great commandments: "Thou shalt love the Lord thy God with all thy heart, and with all thy soul, and with all thy mind, and with all thy strength. This is the first commandment. And the second is like it, namely this,: Thou shalt love thy neighbour as thyself" (Mark 12:30-31). The beauty of nature, the marvellous rhythm of the cosmic flow, and the processes of our own healthy bodies are all fundamentally physical in scale, and yet are also deeply spiritual in content, for they lead the beholder to rejoice in God the creator and sustainer of the universe. Great art, again sensual and physical in its outer manifestation, is man's finest spiritual creation, for it leads the weary soul to its Creator Who is the end of all beauty. Likewise the scientist dedicated to the pursuit of truth is God-centred and spiritually based, for in God is all truth. Those whose lives are devoted to service and care for others are equally spiritual in orientation, for they tread the path of self-giving service in love, and God is above all else love. From this we can deduce that physical communication has strong spiritual overtones when it is inspired by the highest values we know — beauty, truth, and goodness (or love).

The same line of reasoning holds true for psychical communication. When the love of someone dear to us, whether distant in the flesh or in the greater life beyond physical death, lifts us up when we are feeling very low, it is as if God's love is bearing us in His everlasting arms. How often in my own life has such a spontaneous psychical communication from the world beyond space and time (at least as we understand these two modalities of reality) raised me to the greatest felicity when my depression was at its darkest! Great art carries psychical overtones of a deeper level than mere aesthetic delight, and it lifts the obscured soul up to the throne of God. This is why a general denunciation of all psychical communication as diabolical is not only ignorant but also monstrously unjust. The psychical realm, like that of the physical material world in which we live our carnal lives, contains all modalities of value from debased corruption to divine splendour. We are incarnate to redeem, through the love that comes from God, all that is soiled and corrupt so that it may be transfigured and resurrected — following the two great events in the life of Jesus, the Transfiguration and the Resurrection, which relate not only to the life's journey of a God-filled man, but also to the work vouchsafed to all His disciples on the path of Christhood. Just as He descended into Hell to reclaim that which was "lost", so we too have to follow His path. But before we can proceed with safety, we have to "take unto ourselves the whole armour of God" (Ephesians 6:13).

Only the Spirit of God can redeem that which is lost, and this comes to us in the spiritual communication of prayer or of a rapt loss of self in service for others.

Conclusions

To summarise the differences between the psychical and the spiritual, I would say this, that while psychical communication impinges on all aspects of the psyche including the soul, or spiritual self, it only becomes really spiritual when it tells of God Himself in His ineffable mode and reaches the soul from the spirit within it. This is the meaning of mystical experience: it is the experience of union of the soul with God, so that the soul loses itself in Him and finds the spirit within it at the same time. All other types of psychical communication speak to the isolated self, which does not cease from its isolation even when the communication is being given. Some such information can be very beneficial, but other types of communication can be equally demonic in character.

It is for this reason that psychical communication is hazardous, and should not be initiated from the living to the dead. Once psychical communication is thus initiated, it is impossible to predict the nature of the source from beyond the grave which may interfere with and even obsess the dabbler.

No wonder psychical research should be undertaken only by trained, dedicated workers.

4

Survival of Death and Eternal Life

OUR UNDERSTANDING OF the state of being of the deceased personality is obviously highly tentative. Survival of death has never been scientifically proved, for even the most convincing communications from our loved ones on the other side of death can be explained by mechanisms that do not require a survivalistic view of life. This is especially true of mediumistic communication, as I have already noted: much material purporting to come from the deceased does in fact originate in the sitter's mind. However, when the total evidence of alleged communication, whether through mediums of the most irreproachable integrity, such as have been investigated by competent societies devoted to psychical research, or through the much more personally evidential communion between loved ones and friends on either side of the veil of death, is analysed, a very good case for survival of death can be built up. In the end we have to come to our own conclusions; experts can point to pitfalls in the survivalistic hypothesis, but they cannot disprove it categorically.

If survival is a fact, as I strongly believe, it is the psyche which continues when the physical body decays after its death. This psyche, as I have already described, consists of a focal point of personal awareness surrounded by a vast unconscious, the contents of which range from primitive animal drives and painful memories of the past to ennobling drives leading to fulfilment of the person and the vision of God. The psyche of a newly deceased person will, in all probability, not be very different from its condition when it was still associated with the flesh. The confused unconscious material that seeps into awareness during vivid dreams might well be a presage of the sort of early after-life experience in store for many of us when we die.

Heaven and Hell

It has been well said that we make our old age in our youth; a selfish attitude in youth bears its consequence in a selfish, cantankerous elderly person who is loved by few people. On the other hand, a self-giving person may be so open to God's love that he becomes a blessing to others even when he is very old indeed. Such a person grows in spiritual stature even as the years pass, and he begins to look forward to death as a new adventure in his life of self-fulfilment. The enclosed selfish person inherits dark, enclosed imprisonment on the other side of death, and this is the real nature of hell. What we have built up in this life is what we are to inherit in the world beyond death. Similarly, a person who has lived a life of self-giving devotion to others while he was still in the flesh can expect to be greeted with love by those in the greater life beyond death — and those who greet him will not be merely the ones he knew while he was still in the flesh but also the greater communion of saints who guard us and inspire our thoughts with the knowledge of God. This is, in my view, the "judgment" that is in store for all of us when we quit the mortal body: have you been self-centred in your attitude to life or have you been a servant of the highest you know, even God Himself, and shown this devotion to Him by loving your neighbour? The first type of person goes to darkness, the second to light. This is the realm that we call heaven, or paradise. Jesus promised the repentant thief on the Cross with Him that on that very day he would be in paradise with Him (Luke 23:43). Indeed, the thief was already in a heavenly state when he confessed the glory of the One crucified alongside him; even the disciples could not see this glory at that terrible moment. It could be said that the penitent thief was the first Christian believer, for he believed in the humiliated Christ without the evidence of the later glory.

Atonement and Forgiveness

However, the post-mortem state is not the final one. If the person on the other side of death can bear the judgment of his past life and can pray for forgiveness, I have no doubt that he too can rise from the darkness and isolation of hell to the warmth and felicity of heaven. Both those states are of psychic, or mental nature. They are to be seen as a re-living of old attitudes in the light of the greater understanding afforded by a purely psychic mode of experience without the encumbrance of a physical body. If it is objected that I envisage too easy a transition for the penitent sinner from hell to heaven, without the dire eternal punishment threatened in the scriptures, I would say two things. The first is that the transition is slow and extremely painful, for the person is himself one of the judges of his own bad attitudes and actions. To have to confront our inherent sinfulness on this side of life can be distressing enough, as anyone consulting a psychotherapist or a confessor knows full well. A similar confrontation on the other side of life, where there is no physical body to conceal ourselves, is much more painful, for no secrets can be hidden there and all our thoughts and desires are open to the inspection of "all the company of heaven". The second point is that eternal punishment, apart from its contradiction of the love of God for all His creatures, is self-frustrating. What is eternal can have no end, and therefore there can be no hope of redemption for the sinner.

It is unfortunate that the scriptures so often threaten a vindictive punishment for sinners, a punishment conditioned entirely by human understanding of penal reward. There is in fact only one punishment that has any reality: separation from the love of God. And this is never initiated by God, whose nature it is always to have mercy, but by man, who through his gift of free will can actively exclude himself from the love of God. Until man repents, God cannot fill him with the living warmth that comes from His Holy Spirit. But when the light of repentance dawns, itself the result of the terrible suffering borne in the cold isolation of hell and an inner awareness of God's grace, God moves any distance to reclaim the sinner.

However, forgiveness is only the first stage of real salvation, or healing. What we have done wrong has now to be restored, for our own sake as well as that of those whom we have injured. The atonement wrought by Jesus' sacrificial death and passion reconciles man to God, for God was in Christ reconciling the world to Himself (2 Corinthians 5:19). There is forgiveness, and this allows us to continue the work of restoration and reconciliation without remorse or self-destructive feelings of guilt. It is now the love for those whom we have wronged — and indeed for all the world and for ourselves also — that impels us on to become full persons. While we are unforgiven, whatever movement we may make towards the light is selfish in motivation and therefore condemned to failure at its very initiation. When the motive is disinterested love, we are truly in God's service.

The Spiritual Body

The concept of an extensive psyche existing without form or limitation is difficult for us to envisage on this side of death. St. Paul discusses this difficulty in as great detail as is possible for mortal man in the fifteenth chapter of his first letter to the Corinthians. The body we leave at death is corruptible flesh; the body we assume after death is a spiritual body of such a nature that we cannot describe it with our earthly understanding and language. Esotericists describe a number of "subtle bodies" — of various consistencies between matter and immaterial spiritual substance — which surround and interpenetrate us even while in the flesh, and come more fully into their own when the flesh is no more. They speak of a semi-material "etheric body" which closely surrounds the physical body and is possibly the medium of transference of psychic communication to the physical body. This is said to disintegrate some time after the person dies, and then the psyche is enclosed in a finer "astral body" with emotional characteristics. Then there is a finer "mental body" and a somewhat more rarefied "spiritual body" that ensheaths the soul (or spiritual self), which is far removed from the knowledge of most people while they are on earth. I think this scheme is both correct as far as it goes, and yet at the same time unsatisfactory. If the mind is separate from the brain, as I believe, this suggestion of intermediate subtle bodies might provide a mode of connexion between the two. On the other hand, the existence of such bodies is confirmed only by people with the gift of clairvoyance (it is also an article of faith in theosophical speculation, itself derived largely from Hindu metaphysics). Perhaps psychical research will contribute a more scientific approach to this problem in the future.

A much more impressive view of the meaning of the body is to be found in the theological speculations of A. N. Whitehead and Teilhard de Chardin. They see the body as the complete psychic field of influence of a person, and not merely as the organism of flesh and bones that he inhabits when he is alive on the earth. This is merely the concrete form of a person while he is on earth, just as the man Jesus was an incarnate manifestation of the Christ Who is cosmic in scope and extends beyond time and space, begotten before the foundation of the world. But whereas the full body of Christ embraces the whole cosmos (and transcends it), our feeble bodies are enclosed in a little world of selfishness while we are alive. When we die to the physical body and are redeemed through the love of God, so our new body widens in sympathy and extends in love to embrace other bodies. This is the deeper meaning of the "spiritual body" that we acquire after the limited body of our humiliation has been left behind. It is in the wider participation of psychic life that the spiritual body — no matter how we conceive it, for it is beyond present human understanding even if we adopt the esoteric theosophical view — shows its radiance. The body of an aspiring person on the other side of death is more glorious than the one he has quit, for it brings him more closely within the body of Christ which includes all those who dedicate themselves to His service.

In the person of the risen Christ it would appear that His transfigured, resurrected physical body contributed to the glory of His spiritual body. In our own persons this transmutation and resurrection of the physical body is not to be expected, at least at present, because we are still worldly and selfish in our inner lives. Only one of the stature of Christ can have a physical body capable of spiritual transformation. But we must work towards a resurrection, not only of our own bodies of flesh but of the whole world so that we may fulfil St. Paul's visionary glimpse of ultimate reality, when "the universe itself is to be freed from the shackles of mortality and enter upon the liberty and splendour of the children of God" (Romans 8:21).

Rebirth

It is evident that no man, other than the Incarnate Christ, can achieve this degree of spiritual integration in the course of one life-time on earth. As the psyche progresses in the life beyond death, its composite elements of memory, selfish drives, and inner thoughts are incorporated into the soul (in its exalted context of the spiritual self), which grows in fullness through the experience of its life on earth and the period of meditation upon this experience that it undergoes after death. In due course, further experience in a plane of physical limitation becomes necessary for the further growth of the soul into the full knowledge of God. The psychic milieu of the immediate after-death state is one of inner meditation and learning rather than of active growth. This growth can take place only in an environment where self-giving love in relationships with other people is possible; in other words, sacrifice of self and the suffering that accrues from this is the way of growth to a full knowledge of God. What the nature of the realm of physical limitation is, no one can tell. I have already discussed this problem in connexion with a mystical experience I myself had. Suffice to say that it may entail a reincarnational sequence, or else occur elsewhere in the cosmos, possibly in a type of body of quite a different character to anything we can conceive in our present state of limited understanding. Indeed, too great an emphasis on this aspect of rebirth can lead us away from reality into fruitless private speculations, to which enthusiasts of reincarnation are especially prone. The Catholic teaching about purgatory (an intermediate state of survival between hell and heaven in which there is a progressive purification of the soul) seems to be the right one, provided its scope is widened to include all men, irrespective of religious belief, who are aspiring to the vision of God through living in accordance with the law of love. We are indeed in purgatory even now.

Eternal Life

Eternal life is of quite another order from either the life we know in this world, or the life of the world beyond death of the physical body, or of a rebirth sequence. And yet it inter-penetrates all of them. Eternity is a state of reality, indeed is the full reality, that lies outside the limitation of space or time. It is the reality known in mystical illumination; it is the very life of Christ in His ascended form. When we have lived a life dead to selfishness, in the twinkling of an eye, as St. Paul puts it (1 Corinthians 15:51), we shall be changed and enter a new way of life altogether. This promise is not reserved only for those who have died in the flesh; it is the very present hope of all of us, whether here on earth or yonder past the grave. It is already known to the mystic in a brief glimpse, but I believe that it is to be experienced by all men, and indeed the whole creation, when human consciousness has been raised from the personal self to the spiritual self, and is informed of the spirit within it.

If survival and rebirth have any validity at all, they are to be seen as processes of purgation and growth of the soul into full union with the soul of the cosmos and with God Himself. In this way man will grow progressively into a knowledge of Christ. When the last enemy, which is death, is overcome, all things will be subject to the Word of God (or the Son), who will also be made subordinate to God the Father who made all things subject to him, that God may be all in all (1 Corinthians 15:27-28). The way to eternal union with God is also the way of the Incarnate Christ. To attain eternal life is the goal of man. The Buddhist concept of Nirvana can be equated with the life of eternity. It is very important to understand that eternity is outside time and space (and therefore beyond any concept of duration or finitude); it is a new way of life in which "I live, yet not I, but Christ liveth in me" (Galatians 2:20).

When eternal life is known, all other modes of existence, whether on earth or in the life of the world to come, pale into insignificance. They are put in their proper perspective as places of testing and of temporary rest and recreation before the glory of eternity is revealed to us.

III
Milestones on the Path

1

The Way of Self-Awareness

THE PATH TO life is one that leads away from illusion to reality. The unawakened person identifies himself with his surroundings, his conditioning, and his personal attributes and deficiencies. He does not know of an inner core of true identity, which we have called the personal self, remembering once more that this is the reflection and guide to the spiritual self, or soul, that directs an integrated person.

To know oneself as a focus of unique awareness with a personal capacity for responding to outer circumstances is daunting to many people. They would rather follow in the wake of their fellows and do the thing that is accepted (and therefore "right") than move out into the unknown in a trail blazed with personal integrity. The way of self-awareness comes by the experience of life itself. It is in our responses to a variety of events, especially the ones that are unexpected, that we see ourselves most starkly bereft of those attributes we value most highly. This exterior way towards self-knowledge is much more practical than the way opened by psychological exercises of self discovery based on analytic theory and the practice of meditation.

In my own life I have usually seen myself most revealingly (and also most unfavourably) when I have been taken off my guard by an unanticipated occurrence. It is easy enough to be charming and accommodating to another person when one is at one's ease. It is quite another thing to be civil when one is doing something else or is anxious and depressed. The selfishness that is so much a part of natural man comes out very strongly when he is disturbed in some way, or his equilibrium is shattered.

Self-awareness consists in being able to face oneself as one is, during a particular sequence of events. Self-knowledge is a gradual understanding of the full nature of one's personality with its soul as the centre and place of direction. The way of self-knowledge is the path to life eternal, for one cannot have any considerable understanding of the self that does not include a knowledge of God immanent in the soul also. The journey to the height of reality is also the journey within oneself. And just as one cannot scale the heights without first coming to terms with the rubble that litters the foot-hills, so one cannot come to the pearl of great price, the soul, that lies deep within each of us until one has first encountered, mastered, and transmuted the dark elements of the unconscious that obscure the inner light. It is in the moment of self-awareness, which should be every moment of our lives if we were living abundantly, that the whole range of our personality is laid bare before us. What we see may not, in the first instance, be very attractive, but if we persist we are shown that we are even now in the form of eternal life.

Recollectedness

It is a well recognised discipline of the spiritual life that a period should be spent each night in recollection of what we have done, and how we have comported ourselves during the day. This period of recollection brings us back to the way we have revealed ourself to others (and ourself) during the stress of relationships, and as such gives us a useful self-portrait of how we stand at the moment. This discipline should not be regarded as one of morbid introspection or a painstaking analysis of possible motives for every action we have performed. God alone can judge the heart; we have to consider the action itself and what it shows us about ourselves. The practice of awareness in everyday life is one way of developing a conscious response to the details of our surroundings instead of moving around in the witless state of a sleepwalker which too often characterises unawakened man. Nevertheless, this type of exercise in willed awareness and response is tiring and mechanical; in itself it will eventually wane through sheer fatigue and boredom.

This same criticism applies to those schools of inner development which teach their disciples to think and observe themselves carefully before they say or do anything. If this advice were carried out to the letter, the person would lose his spontaneity and his capacity for lightning changes in conduct that may follow fluctuations in outer circumstances. The right way to cultivate self-awareness is to act spontaneously as the situation demands, and then later to meditate quietly and earnestly on that response. Was it part of my desired reaction to such a situation? If not, how did it betray my good intentions, and why did I do it? A few fairly mundane experiences of this type can shatter the imposing façade of learning or respectability we have built around ourselves (Jung's "persona", or mask), and reveal depths of fear, envy, jealousy, and resentment that are seldom confronted directly. The important point is that we of ourselves cannot know, in our present state of development, what is our best way of progress in life. Certainly it is possible to develop a particular aptitude or talent by painstaking practice, but life, and how best we are to live it, is above any personal cultivation.

There is, indeed, only one aim worth considering in life, and that is to become a person, authentic in uniqueness and full of the Spirit of God in fellowship. Material success is in itself to be regarded as a by-product of proper living; while not to be disparaged, it is only an incident on the way towards the fulfilment of the whole person.

Vocation and Self-Fulfilment

How often in one's early years does one aim at emulating the success of someone else who acts as an ideal model! Sometimes the society in which one lives foists this model upon one, and for a considerable time one may really believe one is happy in this role. But the time will come when one's true identity asserts itself, often forcibly and with little finesse, and disrupts the façade that has been erected around oneself. There are, in this respect, two approaches to inner authenticity. One approach lies in following a particular way of life, be it professional or religious, from one's earliest years of decision and carrying on to the end with perseverance. The other approach, which is much less comfortable and satisfactory in respect of the world's demands for compliance, consists in following an inner impulse that leads to the fulfilment of oneself. This is a way that promises no certain outer security, but may bring in its train a fully integrated person. Neither approach is to be seen as the right one except in relation to the person himself. The faithful adherence to a chosen way of life can be justified only if his decision is accompanied by a sense of vocation — a calling from the Spirit to follow the path in faith to the glory of that path and of the One Who is that path. If the way is chosen for motives of crude selfishness and a demand for security, one will quite literally, if one is successful, gain the whole world at the expense of one's true self. On the other hand, following an inner impulse that leads to no certain destination or reward at the outset can be justified only if the real desire of the person is towards exploring the deep things of God. In such a way much of his inner nature will be revealed in the search, and he will be more aware of the spirit within him. But if there is no inner drive towards meaning, the life of such a person will drift aimlessly into feckless self-indulgence and all too easily end in corruption.

Self-Acceptance

This is why the way of self-awareness is really the way of attunement to the Holy Spirit. Amongst the properties of the Spirit is that of leading us into all truth. The first truth to be learned is the position of the person as he now stands. The Spirit is to lead us into truth and wholeness, unlike our unredeemed personal will which is concerned with security and superiority over others. We learn by seeing ourselves as we really are — in work, in difficult relationships, in danger, in illness, and approaching death. We cannot prepare for these effectively by any act of assertive will. We have rather to trust and to act, and in the expression of that action see ourselves in our nakedness. Then comes the period of recollection, which is really a personal extension of the confession of sin that plays an important part in all the world's higher religions.

Of ourselves we cannot alter our adverse response to difficult situations; indeed, such a change would, on this level, be one of unconcealed self-seeking. Even if we chastised ourselves for losing our temper in a taxing situation, or behaving uncharitably when we should have flowed out in succour to someone in need, there is every probability that we still behave inadequately in the future, even if we resolve to check ourselves by intensive self-observation beforehand. The reason is that the motive is impure and selfish: it is the "image" we are projecting that disturbs us rather than our own inner corruption, which is known only to us and to God. By an act of personal will I can regulate my outer activities so as to deceive not only other people but also myself as to my true nature. I may certainly become more efficient and materially successful, but I am further away from my centre than ever.

If, on the other hand, I acknowledge the darkness that is mine and lift it up to God in prayer, He will, through His healing grace, effect an inner transformation of my psyche, so that I will be driven by love and compassion for others and not by motives of self-improvement. The human mind has great difficulty in accepting the free, boundless grace of God; it can only accept that for which it pays. This is part of the terrible sin of pride. The Parable of the Publican and the Pharisee is a perfect demonstration of this spiritual law: the one who is mighty in his own estimation and whose rectitude shines before men believes that his external actions have justified him, and yet he has no love in his heart. The one who is miserable and abased has no outer attribute to justify him and is derelict before his Maker; he shall be filled with good things because he, realising his lack and free from all pride, is ready to receive them. The love of God fills his soul, and his actions will from henceforth flow from him in unceasing love for others. Love is never dammed up or reserved, but flows with the Holy Spirit to the ends of the world.

Self-Love

The paradox about self-awareness is that once we have achieved it we should let it go. It is far removed from the self-consciousness of the selfish man grasping for material or spiritual gifts to boost the self that he really hates, or that of the neurotic person enslaved by the imagined contempt of others for the self that he despises. It is the way towards self-acceptance and a gratitude to God that we are as fully ourselves as He has made us, defects included no less than gifts and talents. This is what is meant by self-love, a love that we are instructed to afford our neighbours equally as ourselves. Once we can accept ourselves as we are and can love our life as we find it, we can move progressively from self-concern to concern for others, until the moment of supreme sacrifice comes when we are able to give up ourselves entirely for the highest we know — love of the brethren and of God. And it is then that we pass from the death of self-centredness to the eternal life of the Spirit (1 John 3:14).

Dreams and Self-Awareness

During sleep the conscious self lies dormant, and the contents of the unconscious are able to escape its censorial power and make themselves known to us in dreams. We now know through neurological research that dreaming is an integral part of the process of sleep, but only sporadically do our dreams make a sufficiently strong impression for us to remember them. Some people have a very active dream-life, while others deny dreaming altogether.

To the aware person a dream can be a vivid pointer to the state of the submerged psyche from where arise the drives that dominate our conscious life. Often the dream is an obvious reaction to some particular situation in which we find ourselves, but even then it has something to tell us about our deeper attitudes and fears. We are much closer to the truth about ourselves when we dream than when we are fully conscious and in a position of vantage; indeed, the two great moments of truth when we really begin to know ourselves are during an unexpected crisis and when we are asleep to the world but awake to the psychic realm, which includes not only our own unconscious but also the collective unconscious of the human race and the psyche of those outside our private realm, even in the life beyond death.

Much dream material presents itself to us in symbols, and

the various schools of psychodynamic theory have their own schemes of interpreting these symbols. The fact that there are different modes of interpreting dreams tells us that there is no final true interpretation that does not come from the person himself. If we can afford the patience and work necessary to record and analyse our more vivid dreams, we will achieve not only self-awareness but also self-knowledge. In my own life I spent a number of years with a group of like-minded seekers, discussing and analysing our various dreams according to Jungian principles. I found the experience liberating and reassuring, but there came a time when I knew that this approach to self-awareness had fulfilled its purpose, at least as far as I was concerned. In my experience the most useful dreams have been those that related to a present circumstance or a past memory and showed that my unconscious reaction to these was at variance with my conscious attitude.

When I have felt assured about my rectitude over certain matters, I have very frequently had a deflating dream that has shown me how weak and unsure I really was of my own case. When I have felt enmity towards others, a corrective dream has shown me all too clearly that I was far from blameless in the matter. The shadow that represents the dark, earthy part of our personality, and may even appear demonic to our well-bred, conscious selves, is often clearly delineated in dreams. And it has to be accepted and loved before the psychic energy it commands can be properly integrated into the personality. But there are often a number of trends even in a single dream; what may be reactive to a present situation may also indicate a hidden attitude, and furthermore include material to be experienced in the future. This precognitive aspect of dreams emphasises their psychic content, and I personally believe that our dream life prepares us for the early stages of the life that follows death of the physical body.

It is for these reasons that no one other than the dreamer himself can give an authoritative interpretation, though the findings of psycho-analysts, especially the Jungians, who are the most broadly based of the various schools, can be of great help, for many symbols are of archetypal significance, having been in general psychic currency since man first came to himself. While it is important not to be obsessional in our quest after dreams, we should make written notes at once — for dreams are very fleeting and are easily forgotten — of those that haunt us when we awaken from our sleep. If the meaning is obscure it is wise to meditate on the dream in silence. In that silence one should pray that the meaning may be revealed. If we wait patiently we will seldom be disappointed, and when the meaning is shown, it will usually astound us by its forthrightness and simplicity.

As I have already said, there usually comes a time when this type of painstaking analysis becomes unnecessary. This coincides with increasing personal integration, but even then we will experience occasional dreams of great magnitude that demand attention and elucidation. Like all other activities, dream analysis can become a dangerous habit if undertaken to the exclusion of all else. Many punctilious dream recorders are self-centred and introspective. In the spiritual life balance and discrimination are essential, and one's dream life must always be complemented by active life in the world at the same time. This means caring for others, and not being immersed only in oneself. There are those who deny ever having dreams, but I suspect that when they move in the direction of greater personal authenticity, their unconscious life will move also and flower into a real revelation of their personality. For the Christian, the Bible is a great treasury of dreams and visions and their interpretation. From Jacob and Joseph through Daniel to Peter and Cornelius there is a golden thread of psychic understanding that the aspirant would do well to reflect on.

In this respect it is useful to distinguish between a dream and a vision. Dreams come to us when the conscious mind and the body are asleep, whereas visions are revelations that appear from the superconscious when the person is fully awake, indeed so awake that he no longer functions from the personal self but rather from the spiritual self. Information of cosmic dimensions may be imparted in this state, which is related to mystical awareness inasmuch as in both the consciousness has moved from the personal self to the spiritual self. But there is no experience of union, which is the acid test of mysticism. The visions of Isaiah (6:1-8) and Ezekiel (1:4-28) are the very impress of the transcendent God on the human soul and form the point of contact between visionary and mystical experience. They speak not of the person's condition but of the person's duty and work in the service of God. In other words, a true vision has cosmic dimensions, whereas a dream is predominently personal in scope, though it too can have highly spiritual overtones. Dreams and visions are both dramatic manifestations of the psychic realm of life, and are ways of showing us our relationship with all created things and with God.

2

The Way of Suffering

WE SUFFER WHEN our personalities are in malalignment with
the will of God, Whose law is union in love with Himself and
all His creatures. Suffering began when God granted man free
will, so that man could see himself apart from God as well as
one with Him. What we call the Fall was man's descent from
idyllic union with God into the world of manifold forms where
separation was the order of creation. The more I consider the
parable of Adam, Eve, and the serpent, who symbolises the
dark subterranean forces of self-assertiveness in the human
psyche, the more I realise how necessary the Fall was for man
to recognise and realise the divinity that God had implanted in
Him. Only if the supreme gift of free will had been withheld
would man have stayed immutably fixed to his creator. But the
love of God is such that He willed his creatures to become full
of their own being, so that they could respond to His love as
friends and not as puppets. It is in this context that Jesus'
farewell discourses to His disciples have particularly moving
poignancy: "You are my friends, if you do what I command
you. I call you servants no longer; a servant does not know
what his Master is about. I have called you friends, because I
have disclosed to you everything that I heard from my Father"
(John 15:15). It is hardly too great a simplification to place the
whole burden of man's path to abundant life on the development of his will in harmony with the will of God.

The Origin of Suffering

Malalignment is an ever-present reality. We are out of harmony with our fellow men, each seeking his private advantage at the expense of the other. We are all out of harmony with the world we inhabit because man exploits nature instead of cultivating and cherishing it. The world itself is out of harmony with the cosmic flow of life and is subject to many "natural disasters". And yet all creation is striving to know its own identity, to find an eternal meaning that transcends the world of change in which it is incarcerated during the life of the flesh. Suffering is both a manifestation of the alienation of the creature from its creative source, and the way of knowing and attaining its true identity.

It is a measure of God's love to us that He does not interfere directly in our lives and solve our difficulties for us. Instead he treats us with infinite courtesy, strengthening us if we ask, but never invading our private sphere of activity. If He were to behave "supernaturally", as He could do at will, all travail and suffering could be removed from the world, but His creatures would become mere ciphers that obey the voice of their Master automatically, without love or dedication. God wants the heart, which is the point of the body where action is fertilised by compassion and love. As a man thinks in his heart, so is he (Proverbs 23:7).

Suffering is here to teach us about the heart and how it may be cultivated. Until the heart is awake, there can be no effective prayer life, only a superficial type of intellectual meditation.

The Meaning of Suffering

The way of suffering is hard and unremitting. It aims at no less than a complete cleansing of the personality from all the unconscious elements that obscure the uncreated light of the Holy Spirit that radiates from the centre of the soul, which is our own spirit. Every experience in relationships with others is a little suffering. For in exposing ourselves to the scrutiny of the unfeeling glance of another person, we are shriven of some clinging conceit. There is no understanding of love that does not demand prior suffering. We suffer not only because we are out of alignment with the soul within us, but because the world is also out of alignment with "eternal nature," which is the "body" or the "glory" of God, or "the uncreated heaven" — terms that hail from the mystical theology of Jakob Boehme. The very idea of personal salvation is inconceivable in a world that has fallen from the primeval splendour of God — thanks to the selfishness of its creatures (Romans 8:18-25) — into the flux of growth, decay, and death, with the ever-present hope of rebirth of all levels (physical, psychical, and spiritual). We who take the glory of the world — its natural beauty and fecundity — for granted, must also learn to accept its darkness and bestiality, which accrue in no small measure from the unre-deemed darkness of the human psyche, just as the pinnacles of art and science which adorn human life derive from the peaks of human creativity.

Until the heart is exposed and cultivated, suffering is barren and meaningless, but once the heart expands and beats in understanding, it suffers to the glory of God in the redemption of the world. By this I mean that suffering accepted passively as a personal misfortune neither enlightens the mind nor ennobles the soul. The person himself is bowed down under its weight, mute and hostile. Eventually he will collapse under the burden and die, if not cursing God as Job's wife advised (2:9), at least with bovine incomprehension. There is no call to sentimentalise suffering or to glorify it for its own sake. On the contrary, it calls for amelioration and relief, so that the sufferer may know that others care about him, and that the world at large sees itself as part of a suffering community.

Suffering that opens the heart of the victim at once frees him from self-pity and isolation into a world of greater understand-ing where suffering is the shared mark of all servers on the way. As soon as suffering evokes compassion, the victim is no longer alone in his own imagination, but has left his little self behind and is participating in the life of the world. It is the strange nature of man that, in his prosperity and success, he tends to become self-centred and aloof from the feelings of his fellows, but once he has been brought low, he is able to identify himself with them. And in this state of silent identification,

God Himself can at last gain entry into what is in reality His own domain, but which He has given unreservedly to self-willed man. Of all the ways of attaining mystical experience, it is the one of identification through suffering that is the most exalted, because it tells of love in a fashion that no other mode of approach to the divine can. It is man's duty and his joy to suffer in the image of Christ until all that is corrupt, astray, and lost can be reclaimed, redeemed, and sanctified.

No one on the path of discipleship can avoid the experience of suffering; anyone who tries to evade it by occult techniques fails to reach the end of his journey. "Any one who does not enter the sheepfold through the gate, but gets in some other way is a thief and a brigand. The one who enters the gate is the shepherd of the flock; the gatekeeper lets him in, the sheep hear his voice...the sheep follow because they know his voice. They never follow a stranger but run away from him; they do not recognise the voice of strangers" (John 10:1-5).

There is no journey to the end that is not also the journey with Everyman. By our stripes he is healed. We suffer that he may know our forgiveness, and we learn about our true identity and its consummation into a full person when we suffer on the way.

Suffering and Identity

I once knew a woman of great innate nobility. Her heart was pure but her personality was awry. Her body was very beautiful, but her intellect was not strong. At times she had glimpses of reality, but all too often her vision was clouded by trivialities — what she should do to assert her station in life, how she should prevent others taking advantage of her, how she should retain a proper image of herself (as much for her own stability as to impress others). If anyone crossed her or she suspected she was being snubbed, there would commence a bitter feud that might last years on end. And it was all so trivial; she had so much that ought to have gratified her. But she did not know herself.

Her bitter tongue ruined many relationships, yet those who had suffered were eventually able to forgive her, divining the nobility and compassion that lay beneath the unstable surface.

She clung desperately on to what she loved, but as we all have to learn, there comes a time when we have to relinquish everything, as she found out. The last few years of her life were dark, and eventually she fell victim to an incurable internal disease. At last she began to come to herself. All her friends and relations rallied round her, each visiting her out of love and giving her beautiful presents which she knew intuitively she would never be able to use. Suddenly the realisation struck her; "What a nasty person I have so often been. I wonder why all these people are so good to me." She began to see the reality of her life as something apart from the façade of physical beauty or social eligibility that had so often dominated her thoughts when she was young. At last she understood that she was loved for what she was, and not for what people might get out of her. This was the moment of truth in a very pathetic life. Now she was prepared to pass beyond the gate of death to the life beyond it.

When she died she was young and beautiful to behold, though in fact she was sixty years old.

Suffering and Forgiveness

There was a man who seemed to have many misfortunes borne on him. He was an unloved child who came of an intensely religious household, and much was expected of him. Indeed, his sights were aimed at so great a height by his unimaginative, decorous parents that he had no chance of ever fulfilling their hopes. What little initiative he had was soon obliterated by the strife and turmoil of school, and being a person of modest intelligence, he could never assert himself. This basic physical impotence showed itself later in a failure to get the right work and to form a durable relationship with a woman. By middle age he was severely neurotic, and at last could see the terrible havoc his parents' attitude and upbringing had wrought on him. An overwhelming hatred for them consumed him, for he knew now that his life was ruined, and stark failure confronted him.

In his hatred he became aggressive and violent, so much so that at one point he fell foul of the law and was brought up before the magistrate, who cautioned and discharged him. This event was the turning-point in his life. Timid at heart, he was shocked both at his violence and hatred and at the threat of imprisonment that had impinged itself so closely upon him.

It was fortunate for him that, at this stage of his life, he was brought into contact with a group of Christians who practised meditation together using Biblical themes. Their religion was open and undogmatic, and in their company this warped man could at last gain a little inner peace. He began to see that the resentment he felt against society for the worldly success, and all that followed from it, that had been denied him, was childish and immature and that real living was giving of oneself to others. He started, in the company of the other members of the group, to visit and assist the sick and the blind. At first this was a severe imposition on him, for he gained no material benefit from it. And yet his life had gradually started to gain some meaning. He was able to subsist on a meagre salary doing uninspiring work, but at last his self-esteem rose by degrees.

Slowly he realised that the noblest purpose of life is service to one's fellow men, service that can demand nothing in return, but bestows on him who gives it a greater knowledge of the love that comes from on high. His heart was now opened to that love, and he ceased to fear and loathe (the two are really one) his aged parents and began to feel compassion towards them, and indeed towards all people. As the years passed this man was able to make a happy marriage, and to venture forth into more fulfilling work. He was, admittedly, not very successful financially, but his life flowered into ever greater peace and forgiveness. He had found the pearl of great price within himself through being bereft of all those external conceits that the world esteems most highly. Suffering had opened his heart to the love of God Who forgave him and healed his personality. At last he could live with single-minded purpose, being himself and not merely losing himself in a superfluity of good things.

Suffering and Enlightenment

It is one thing to suffer because of a lack of personal enlightenment, but what about those seekers on the path who have to suffer the supreme deprivation of having their "faith" cut away from under their feet! My own life, so much that of an outsider (but also one with Jesus Who is the eternal outsider — outside all the limits and dimensions that the world has erected, and even those within which the Church that has arisen in His name has vainly tried to imprison Him), has brought me frequently into contact with those who believe they have lost their faith. At one time everything was cut and dried; they knew they had been "saved," that the Lord had a definite work for them to do each day, that it was their duty to show others also the way to salvation. Their life was a prolonged holiday with the Almighty; all they had to do was obey the basic commandments and all would go well with them! Yet somehow the vision had grown dim. The assurance that was once so strong had waned, and experiences in their life had taught them, as Job had also to be taught, that God was not so easily defined as they had imagined, and that the action of the Holy Spirit was more free than any person could divine. In this state of spiritual darkness, which is the contemporary counterpart of the dark night of the soul so well described by many medieval Christian mystics, there are two possible sequels: cynical despair that leads to self-destruction and suicide (at least on a psychical level) or self-discovery through a greater openness to the uncharted providence of God. It is the latter way that comes of the Holy Spirit, and it shows itself in the development of new insights and new faculties.

This is indeed one of the most rewarding features of the contemporary spiritual scene. Those who were limited by fixed, conventional religious views (often described pejoratively as orthodoxy, a word which should embrace the proper glorification of God as well as the right doctrine) are having their perspectives widened by the inflow of the ceaselessly active Holy Spirit, the lord and giver of life. The rather spectacular, and to my mind superficial, Charismatic Movement is certainly a liberating force in the current Christian scene, and could be the presage of a much deeper, more penetrating mystical transformation provided its adherents do not try to quench the Spirit by limiting the full force of His renewing grace. But the Spirit blows in other directions also. It may be necessary for some highly conservative Christians to make contact not only with the Hindu-Buddhist metaphysic and systems of meditation to broaden their own spiritual perspectives, but also to learn more about psychical and mystical levels of awareness.

On the other hand, those who tend strongly towards esoteric and occult systems of training — and in my opinion including even the Hindu-Buddhist group — will never attain full liberation until they take on themselves the yoke of suffering that comes from the incarnate Jesus Christ. "Come unto me, all ye that labour and are heavy laden, and I will give you rest. Take my yoke upon you, and learn of me: for I am meek and lowly in heart; and you shall find rest unto your souls. For my yoke is easy, and my burden is light" (Matthew 11:28-30).

From all this we can begin to derive a new concept of faith, which also is a gift of the Holy Spirit. It is the ability to be open to new possibilities, to know that the world is intrinsically good, having been made by God, Who saw that everything was very good when He made it (as the first chapter of the Book of Genesis declares), and which cannot be permanently corrupted by any action of the creature who governs the world, even man.

Suffering and Pride

Pride is the antithesis of faith. It is indeed the cardinal sin. All the other sins are subordinate to it. The proud man is full of himself; he cannot let go of himself, for if he did, his little domain would disintegrate. He cannot entertain faith for anything outside himself. The fruit of pride is clearly suffering, for the proud man cannot align himself to anybody else, let alone the cosmic flow of God.

But pride goes before the inevitable fall, and then God's grace can enter the shattered personality, which is at last receptive to the healing agencies that derive from God — whether medical, psychological, or psychical. It is no over-simplification to say that all suffering accrues from personal pride. Admittedly even the humble person — and the humility I speak of is not a self-centred recital of sins and faults, but an open receptivity to the love of God — who is full of faith as I have defined it, does not escape harsh affliction in this world.

The Lord did not tell Dame Julian of Norwich that she would
have no more difficulties with which to contend, but He did
assure her that she would never be overcome (*Revelations of
Divine Love,* Chapter 68). There is, however, a subtle difference
between bearing an affliction and suffering personally. In the one
there is the knowledge that God is with us, and we are "putting
on the new man" as St. Paul would say (Ephesians 4:24;
Colossians 3:10). In the sufferings of everyday life it is the "old
man", the personal self and the psyche, that is wounded. And
how he kicks against the pricks! When Jesus bore our afflictions
He experienced the personal suffering, and the resentment that
flowed from it, of the whole creation (and especially man). But
He did not complain or revile His Father. St. Paul sees this
bearing of the world's suffering as the work of the fully realised
Christian; "I now rejoice in my suffering for you, and fill up that
which is behind of the afflictions of Christ in my flesh for his
body's sake, which is the church" (Colossians 1:24).

It should be noted finally that pride is not the same thing as
self-esteem. If we do not esteem ourselves, there is no hope for
us at all. As I have written earlier, self-acceptance is a part of
the spiritual journey, for when we can really know and love
ourselves as we are, we will also begin to know and love our
neighbour, who is every man we meet. Self-esteem is a
conscious acknowledgment of the uniqueness of our own
person — and therefore of the unique value of all other persons
also. Pride is an enclosed, imprisoned view of the person that
prevents the inflow of God's love, which alone can transform
and renew the personality.

Suffering and Cosmic Disasters

These is, of course, a type of suffering which follows what
we call "natural disasters," such as floods, cyclones, earth-
quakes, and volcanic eruptions. There are described as "acts of
God" in insurance parlance. But are they really God's
responsibility?

Here we are in the field of pure speculation of course, but it
is not beyond the bounds of possibility that malign psychic
forces that proceed from corrupt evil men and societies have
their effect even on the weather and the structure of the earth.

Just as destructive poltergeist activity can develop in the vicinity of a psychologically unbalanced person — usually an adolescent with strong psychic powers — is it not possible that such activity on a greatly magnified scale could have cosmic repercussions, especially if those who have passed beyond the veil of death into the life of the world to come, add their quota of psychic emanations to the general cosmic chaos?

As I have already admitted, this is merely a speculation, but it is worth considering very deeply. The converse effect would be produced by those who are balanced, integrated persons. Their calming, healing influence is well recognised on a personal level. If more people were to emulate their example, perhaps the earth itself would be a more harmonious planet, less susceptible to natural disasters.

I have already quoted St. Paul on the sufferings of the world following the selfishness of its creatures (Romans 8:18-25). But he also describes a vision of the world liberated from the shackles of mortality to enter into the glorious liberty of the children of God (verse 21).

3

The Inner Way — Meditation

As WE PROGRESS on the path of life we become increasingly aware of our own insufficiency. We are, however, able to call with greater trust on that power beyond us — and also within us — which we call God.

The Fact of God

No man has ever encountered God directly, for none, save the Son of God made flesh, could survive the meeting: the spiritual power released would destroy the creature. I find too often that people who affirm with great assurance their belief in God are in fact worshipping an image of Good that they themselves have constructed. It is easy enough to define God according to those attributes we especially revere, but God is far beyond any attribute that we can imagine, for He is the source of all attributes. The Christian affirms the presence of God in the Incarnate Christ, but even this impeccably orthodox statement, irreproachable as far as it goes, can, in some quarters, tend to limit the qualities of Christ, Who was assuredly incarnate in the form of a man that was crucified and resurrected. But He, in His cosmic form, is the eternal Word and Wisdom of God, active before the foundation of the world, and at the same time the light that enlightens every man, as St. John states in the prologue of his gospel.

It is therefore not to be wondered at that the spiritually aspiring person is considerably less dogmatic in his views about God than is the conventional religionist. To be less certain about God's nature is a sign, not of unbelief but of the humility that is the prerequisite for a further revelation of God's grace. As we grow into full humanity, our faith deepens, but we cease to see God exclusively in a personal mode, speaking only to our condition. We begin to know more about a Being that transcends limited personality and is in communion with all creation. This is the transpersonal manifestation of God. The world's great mystics, of all the religious traditions, affirm the unknowability of God, Who in His fullness is best defined in negative terms; any positive assertion limits God. For in Him all things co-inhere. He is the point of coincidence of all that is contradictory. If we try to grasp Him intellectually, He will move beyond the ambit of our mind. All we will possess is a vapid image of our own devising. It is for this reason that the fullness of the Deity is best contemplated in terms that transcend personality. The concept of the Godhead, used especially by that very great Christian mystic, Meister Eckhart, is helpful; as this is beyond the terms of human understanding, the pronoun "It" is best used for descriptive purposes. But this does not degrade the Godhead to the impersonal status of an object; it exalts the Godhead above the limitation of personality to transpersonal communion with all creatures.

The paradox of the situation is this: while the rational mind at its peak of understanding cannot comprehend God, the quiet mind can be receptive to the grace of God Who approaches it in the form of personality. In other words, when we are silent and at peace in ourselves, God can come to us and make Himself known to us as a person among persons. It is thus that we can identify God by the personal pronoun He, though the stress on masculinity implicit in that pronoun is unfortunate in its exclusiveness. It can be deduced from this that in the form of eternal life God is beyond attributes, but in the world of time and space — the world of becoming — God shows Himself to us in terms of personality. The principal manifestation of personality is love, and this is how God reveals Himself to the receptive soul, whether during contemplation or in the purposeful activity of work in the world. We know God by His outflowing energies while we are persons. The mystic who has transcended private personality sees God as the infinite reality, better contemplated in terms of the void or the endless one than as a finite being. We indeed know God according to our own state of self-knowledge and maturity.

As we transcend private personality — the mode of self-concern and self-interest — and put on the collective personality of the world, so we become full persons; as such we gain understanding about the person of God, a very different person to that grasped by the unrealised man. It is in this form that the persons of the Holy Trinity may be well glimpsed. In the Godhead is the eternal generation of the Trinity: the Father Who creates, the uncreated Son by Whom all substantive creation is evoked as the Word and Wisdom of God, and Who is also the Redeemer of all that is fallen and awry, and the Spirit that effects creation by infusing all creatures with life, and sanctifies their redeemed wills so that they can return to the Father as full persons, responsible and free.

If the knowledge I have described is to come to us, we have to be quiet, humble, and open to receive it. The act of becoming quiet and receptive to the power of God is called meditation. In its most simple context meditation is a state of mental repose in which extraneous impressions from the world around us and from our own unconscious can be stilled and eliminated. At this stage the mind is quiet and relaxed and is ready to assimilate knowledge from realms of existence that far transcend the limited world of the five senses. In order to meditate there are no metaphysical or religious pre-requisites; indeed, a non-theist can often meditate effectively on the void of silence, while an atheist may find great bodily relaxation and mental renewal from the shared silence.

It is unfortunate that meditation is now such a popular practice that it tends to be seen as something apart from the world of everyday life, rather than as the essential way of constructive living. If our minds were quiet and untroubled, we would be able to concentrate fully on the work on hand and act with greater efficiency and in harmony with others also. In such a state of conscious receptivity we would be open to inspiration from sources far beyond our usual range, and we would be able to imagine creatively. Creative imagination is the means whereby new hypotheses, whether scientific or philosophical, flash into our minds, where they are clothed in thought and made intelligible to other people. By creative imagination the beauty of form, sound, and word that is inherent in "eternal nature" (the world of eternal values that is unsullied by the creature) comes down to the individual mind where it is transcribed into the plastic arts, music, and literature. By creative imagination God shows Himself to us in vision and illumination, and we in turn transmit this illumination in the form of mystical theology— the only theology that is authentic, for it comes from the Spirit and not merely from the mind of man ("The letter killeth, but the Spirit giveth life" — 2 Corinthians, 3:6).

The Practice of Meditation

To write about the practice of meditation would seem superfluous in view of the plethora of literature on this subject. In fact, meditation cannot be understood from even the most inspired description; its meaning dawns only in the practice of silence in the presence of fellow seekers. In my own work, I encourage those new to the discipline first of all to put their body at ease by consciously acknowledging each limb and part in turn and being grateful for its presence. Special attention to breathing is useful at the outset in order to achieve relaxation of the abdomen by diaphragmatic breathing, but as soon as this relaxation is achieved, I encourage the meditator to forget about his breathing altogether.

Relaxation of the emotions and intellect is more difficult. One way of obviating these tensions is to instruct the meditator to rest his mind on a particular phrase or word that is repeated over and over again until the word vibrates in harmony with the person's own inner rhythm. Personally I do not use this technique, for I believe that the emotions and intellect must not be by-passed, but rather brought into the meditation, just as the relaxed body is also glorified in its own way. I therefore try to evoke feelings of gratitude, thanksgiving, and peace in the meditator — gratitude for the opportunity to be able to set aside a little time for meditation in the course of a hectic daily life, thanksgiving that we are all together in a suitable place and are, at least for this brief period, in physical safety and security, and peace at least during the period when we are all one together. Indeed, although we may have come from a taxing situation and may have to return to it later on, we can at least be at peace one with another during the period of quiet. It is possible, in fact, to use such themes as peace, thanksgiving, and serenity as subjects for meditation, and move progressively into them in complete self-abandonment. Alternatively, when there is such inner quiet, the mind may be filled with a great scriptural theme such as Isaiah's vision in the Temple (Isaiah 6:1-8), Moses' vision of the burning bush (Exodus 3:1-6), Job's encounter with God (Job 38:1-7), some of the Psalms (such as 19, 23, and 121), the Transfiguration (Mark 9:2-8), the walk to Emmaus (Luke 24:13-32), or the Ascension (Acts 1:6-11). For those of a more agnostic, humanistic temperament, a passage of beautiful poetry or descriptive prose may be an excellent anchor for the mind, or even an imagined scene of natural beauty, such as the ascent of a high mountain or a walk through a still meadow or a forest.

The object of these various themes is not discursive study but unitive contemplation. In other words, one should not analyse the theme with the discursive intellect, an exercise that is tiring and eventually frustrating, so much as identify oneself with it. When subject (the meditator) and object (the theme) are one, the mind has found its rest, and the person has really begun to meditate. There comes a time when the stillness born of this union of subject and object (the I-Thou relationship of Buber carried into the field of inner imagination) infuses the whole person, and a new way of living opens out for him. At this stage there is neither distinctive meditator nor theme, but a new creation: all are one in a reality that transcends form and finitude. It is the Eternal One Who is God. And yet there is no merging or self-annihilation; on the other hand, it is only now that the meditator knows his true self (or spiritual self), which finds its life and integrity in God (in whom we live, and move, and have our being — Acts 17:28). This state of loss of limited self-centredness in the fullness of the formless void where God is known is called contemplation, and it is the link between meditation and prayer.

The death of the old self in service and sacrifice is the way to a knowledge of one's true self, which is eternal in nature. But one cannot die to the old self until it has been acknowledged and used in service — indeed, until it is a worthy sacrifice to God's kingdom. Even Jesus did not give Himself to death on the Cross until He had accomplished His Father's will on earth. This is why the experience of contemplation should not be separated, or divorced, from a proper identification of the person with the world in which he lives in the form of a physical body with a rational mind. In other words, contemplation is an advanced state of the spiritual life, and should come only to those who are integrated enough in personality to receive it. Meditation techniques that induce contemplative silence through the repetition of phrases or words can certainly achieve their object often with surprisingly little difficulty and great rapidity, but if the meditator is not already an integrated, balanced person, it is all too easy for him to lose contact with his own identity and become enmeshed in a diffuse, formless void which he mistakes for God. But this diffuse void actually separates him both from his own true self and from effective communication with his fellows. He becomes increasingly remote from the world where we all have to live, at least in our physical bodies, and less outflowing in social relationships. On the other hand, these techniques can be of considerable value to more experienced aspirants on the way who have found the traditional prayers and liturgies of their particular religious traditions unhelpful in the inward path.

Fruits of Meditation

Meditation is no panacea. It does not remove physical or psychological difficulties, nor does it, on its own, effect moral renewal. If a master criminal were to practise meditation without any moral scruples or spiritual aspiration, he would perform his anti-social work with even greater efficiency than before! If a psychotic person, or one in severe psychological difficulties, were to meditate without expert guidance, his field of consciousness would be swamped with previously repressed psychic material from his loaded unconscious, and a complete mental breakdown might ensue. This applies particularly to techniques that by-pass the emotions and intellect and reach directly to the formless void. Those who are particularly sensitive to psychic influence from outside sources (so-called sensitives, or mediums), can be assailed by various types of communications varying from edifying messages from the deceased to dark, unhappy material from the dead or the living (in the persons of those meditating with them in a group).

I mention these adverse aspects of meditation not to alarm the newcomer but simply to put at his disposal the full facts of the case. In actual practice, meditation is much more often a health-giving mental activity which can lead to spiritual renewal and an augmented prayer life. As in all other activities, the attitude and motive of the person are of crucial importance. Nor can the health of the body and the mind be disregarded. A person who investigates meditation because he is dissatisfied with the surface meaninglessness of his life and longs for a greater understanding of reality is on the right path. If in addition he has intelligent insight into his own character, especially the various moral failings to which we are all heir, he is in a good position to practise meditation. None of us is completely sound psychologically, or upright morally, or healthy physically. But if we can face our defects directly and without prevarication, then we are fit people to venture into meditation. The less self-centred our attitude is, the more easily we can meditate. If self-development is our overriding concern, we will strain for attainment that in fact comes only when we relax in trust and self-giving. If, on the other hand, we meditate to cultivate our inner life for the benefit of the world, especially as a prelude to prayer, our meditation time will be a source of benediction to us and to others.

If meditation is practised assiduously, our personalities will attain balance, and our sense of perspective will widen. In everyday life the mind tends to course unprofitably around obsessions, fears, resentments, and anxieties. The more we identify ourselves with these thoughts and emotions by constantly lapsing into them, the more are we enslaved by them, and the less free is our will to act constructively in any particular situation. On the other hand, meditation helps to clear the mind of emotional debris, so that its vision becomes less clouded and its action more efficient. It is a fact that most of us think far too much and at the same time very inefficiently. We are consumed by vain thoughts and fruitless imaginings. If we were in full command of our intellectual and emotional life, the mind would be still and untroubled. Instead of thinking superficial, unhelpful thoughts, the mind would not think at all; in place of thought there would be receptivity of the mind to the world around us and the pulsating life within us. In this way we would really be aware of things that are both temporal and eternal. When the occasion arose in which detailed planning was necessary, the mind would think coherently and constructively, hindered as little as possible by fears and anxieties arising from the situation.

Jesus said, "Peace I leave with you, my peace I give unto you: not as the world giveth, give I unto you. Let not your heart be troubled, neither let it be afraid" (John 14:27). It is this peace that the disciple attains after meditation; it is also the peace that he should give to the world, even as Jesus gave it to those who would receive it. This is the acid test of effective meditation, that it sheds fresh light in the mind of the meditator about the nature of reality, and that he flows out in that peace that passes all understanding to the world in his daily life.

Meditation in Relationships

A real relationship is a meditation between two people. This is the I-Thou relationship described by Buber. Each has lost his isolation in the other, and both have found a new meaning to life — no longer the mortal life of the flesh but the eternal life of the spirit. The unifying power in such mutual self-giving is love, and it is at this point that meditation gives way to prayer. In pure meditation it is the head that acts; in prayer the heart also acts and flows out in love.

The usual worldly relationship is an I-It affair. When one speaks to another person, one is hardly aware of him as a distinct being in his own right, but simply as a sounding-board for one's own ideas and feelings. But when one becomes silent before the mystery of another human being (or animal, or plant, or inanimate object) and observes in wonder and respect, one is contemplating not only that person (or creature) but also God Who fashioned and created the creature. And then one begins to learn about the Creator, the creature, and oneself also. When we are able to listen in silence to the life story of another person and not respond at once with our own wisdom, a greater wisdom, that of the Holy Spirit who is the Advocate, will flow from our lips and lead both that other person and ourselves into the truth.

From the lips of the silence proceeds wisdom, the Word of God.

From the hushed heart flows love.

4

The Inner Way — Prayer

PRAYER BEGINS WHEN the heart is open in compassion to the world around one, when one has passed beyond self-enclosure to participation in the greater life of the communion of saints. While meditation is possible even for those who have no religious convictions, prayer has validity only for him who believes that there is some form of being that comes as a person in relationship to himself. Prayer is a venture in faith, that all we are and know is in communion with a power that shows itself in the world as love.

Meditation is the way of stilling the mind so that the one thing that alone is needful, the entry of the divine grace into the personality, can be effected. In its most profound form, contemplation, there is rapt communion with God in the eloquent silence of the turbulent void. But there is no commitment of the person to God: what is experienced is a meeting on a very high level of consciousness. Prayer is a consummated meeting in which "we present ourselves as a living sacrifice, holy and acceptable unto God, which is our reasonable service" (Romans 12:1). There is in fact only one quality that we can in some measure give back to God — the love that He first bestowed on us. But when we return it in loving service, that love now bears the impress of our own nature upon it, and it comes to God renewed and vibrant with life. We give ourselves in love to God in prayer, and we are transformed by the healing love of God. From all this it can be seen how necessary a proper, disciplined meditation life is for true prayer to flourish, yet how cold and impersonal meditation can be when compared with the warm response of prayer.

The Mechanism of Prayer

The prime influence and effector of prayer is the Holy Spirit within us (Romans 8:26). We begin to pray quite spontaneously when we realise that there is no person or power in the material universe which can help us. This realisation does not take long to dawn in our consciousness, for in all the really great problems of life we have to take personal decisions and commit ourselves to responsible actions that follow those decisions. There is no one who can give us authoritative guidance; indeed, the wisest counsellor will direct the seeker back on himself to find the appropriate answer to his problem. No person can assume the role of infallible guide or teacher, except the person of God.

The Holy Spirit leads us into all truth once we are in a state of humility, or openness, ready to receive Him, or rather to acknowledge His primacy in our own personality. The first truth to learn is that there is something very wrong with us as we now stand. The state of wrongness is shown by a destructive attitude to the world in relation to our own welfare, and is called "sin" in theological terminology. Sin is man's "natural" state — when the flesh and all that appertains to it dominates his life — and brings him sharply back to his animal inheritance. Whenever we magnify the impulse to self-gratification to the detriment of other people, we are sinning. In an animal such a mode of action is not improper, but in man the innate spiritual nature opposes this tendency and acts to move him away from self-concern towards concern for others, even God, whom only the soul understands, albeit indistinctly. The confession of sin that plays a great part in the Christian tradition seems exaggerated and insincere to many detached observers, but those on the spiritual path know better. Even the advanced aspirant is perpetually balanced on the knife-edge between self-indulgence and selflessness. Often the selfish impulse wins a mental victory, but the Spirit infuses the person with a nobler view of life before the crucial action is performed.

In my own life I am continually being saved from self-betrayal and rank cowardice by the strengthening power of the Holy Spirit Who impels me to choose the nobler alternative even when my personal will is awry and at its most perverse. It is the fruit of an arduous life of prayer that God never leaves one even when one shows oneself inwardly to one's greatest detriment.

Once we are able to face our sin, both as an attitude to life and in its more precise context in our actions, we can lift it up to God Who is known to us as love. Love will forgive us our sin, and start the process of redemption by filling us with divine love also. If we can confront our sinful nature directly, but without either destructive judgment or comfortable excuses, God will heal us and fill us with the love that is His most comprehensible quality. This unreserved love renders sin less necessary and more impossible in the future. The proof of effective prayer is not so much an obvious answer to a request or a petition as the opening out of the fearful, selfish heart in a wave of compassion, so that we begin to see beyond our personal self-interest. "Though our outward man perish, yet the inward man is renewed day by day. For our light affliction, which is but for a moment, worketh for us far more exceeding and eternal weight of glory; while we look not at the things which are seen, but at the things which are not seen; for the things which are seen are temporal; but the things which are not seen are eternal" (2 Corinthians 4:16-18). This is the fruit of prayer, and the way in which it cleanses and heals the personality.

To face the corruption within that the Spirit reveals, and to lift it up to God — who, of course, already knows, since His Spirit is the way-shower — in humility is the substance of prayer. But the heart of prayer is silent communion with God. All thoughts and petitions, whether spoken aloud or enunciated silently, are in effect themes of meditation that bring us close to God in our need and dereliction. But it is the silence that should follow the mental activity, be it petition or praise, which is the way of effective communion with God. Articulated prayer, whether intelligible or in tongues of prasie, edifies the person who prays and effects great emotional release, but in

itself says little to us about God's revelation in the holiest part
of the soul, which is called the spirit. When the mind is stilled
and the heart ardent, then prayer is at its most intimate and we
can say "be still, and know that I am God" (Psalm 46:10).

From all this it follows that enunciated "prayers" which play
such an important part in the liturgy of the Church serve
essentially to quieten the mind and bring it to the foot-hills of
meditation. But the stereotyped articulation of well-known
religious material is far from the spirit of true prayer. This
comes quietly and unobtrusively when the mind is quiet and
the heart aflame with aspiration. It is through the silent
outflow of love, both to God from Whom all blessings proceed
and to our fellow men, that prayer finds its summation. Indeed,
man's supreme act is prayer; in the communion that is prayer
human life is consecrated to God.

The Heart of Prayer

The purpose and meaning of prayer is communion between
the soul and God. To be sure we can never grasp God for this
communion, but can only wait in dedicated silence for Him to
inspire the soul with His presence. He is, of course, eternally
present; it is we who are so seldom at home in ourselves to
receive Him. "When thou prayest, enter into thy closet, and
when thou hast shut the door, pray to thy Father which is in
secret; and thy Father which seeth in secret shall reward thee
openly. But when ye pray, use not vain repetitions, as the
heathen do: for they think that they shall be heard for their
much speaking" (Matthew 6:6-7). In these well-known injunctions about true prayer from the Sermon on the Mount, we
have eternal guide-lines to communion with the Father. The
closet referred to is the sanctuary within us, which is the
spiritual self, or soul, and the door to be shut is that which
communicates with the personal part of the psyche in which
desires, fears, and thoughts make their presence known. In
prayer all these lesser things are banished from our consciousness, as we give ourselves to God alone, who is known to us in
the spirit of the soul where dwells His Holy Spirit. Even the
invocation of the most praiseworthy qualities and elevating
ideas occludes the presence of God from our spiritual vision; at

most, such thoughts serve merely to quieten the mind prior to prayer. But when prayer begins, all images disappear from the mind, which is clear and tranquil.

It is when we are least aware of ourselves as separate individuals that we are closest to God; in the union wrought by prayer we grow into the likeness of God, as revealed in the person of the Incarnate Christ. Healing of the whole person — body, mind, and soul — is the outcome of the divine encounter, so that we may become more Christ-like even in the daily round of mundane life. In the Christian scheme, prayer is offered to the Father through the Son (Who is the image of the invisible God, Colossians 1:15) by the power of the Holy Spirit. The Son is known to us by His eternal indwelling in the soul of man (Christ in you, the hope of glory, Colossians 1:27) as well as by His witness in the person of Jesus. Indeed, it is the Spirit Who proceeds from the Word that is in every man that affirms that Jesus Christ is Lord (Philippians 2:11), for in His life we see most fully the action of God in the flesh of this world. I believe that whosoever prays to the Father is in effect using this scheme of approach, no matter what doubts he may have about the person of Jesus Christ; as the doubter proceeds in life, so the supremacy of Jesus in expressing God's action in the world will become clearer to him. Indeed, the full meaning of Jesus' ministry is still hidden even from the most dedicated Christian; the Christ, both cosmic and incarnate, is larger than the measure of man's mind, especially when that man is full of his own conceit and believes he has the complete answer to the mystery of Christ. "The letter killeth, but the Spirit giveth life" (2 Corinthians 3:6). Whoever dedicates himself to the nobler vision of life is experiencing the Word of God, Who is the indwelling Christ, within his soul, and is being impelled by His Spirit.

It follows from this that the meaning of prayer is union with God. Prayer is the elevation of the mind to God and the dedication of the personality to His service. Petition and intercession are at the foot-hills of the prayer of union, while praise is both the consequence of the act of prayer and a constant accompaniment of it. There is in fact only one petition worth making, that God's will may be done through one. In order that this may be effected, one must be a dedicated servant of God, progressively cleansed of all self-indulgence and delusion. As the weaknesses in our character are transfigured and glorified in the power of strength, so we become more perfect agents of the divine action in the world.

Praying for Others

There is probably no more certain stimulus to one's prayer life, when all is dim and uncertain around one, than a concern for others. Even when one's faith is very low, a duty to other people can be a potent impulse towards persistent prayer. What does intercessory prayer hope to achieve? In the earlier stages of the spiritual path when the personal self of the intercessor is still clamant, there is an arrogant certainty that he knows what is needful for the one in distress. To be sure, it is not difficult for a detached observer to diagnose the spiritual deficiencies of someone else. But it is often the case that these obvious defects are merely superficial indications of a much deeper malady of the personality. If they are "miraculously" cured, it is very likely that even worse difficulties will take their place — indeed, this is one application of the teaching of Jesus about the man who was released of one unclean spirit only to be invaded again by the same spirit and seven others, because the psyche was still unhealed and therefore a fit abode for any psychic disturbance (Matthew 12:43-45).

As one progresses in spiritual understanding, so one becomes less intent on forcing one's own views and panaceas on other people. Instead, one simply flows out in love and compassion to them, trusting that the Holy Spirit will perform His life-giving work of resurrecting the ailing personality. This is the secret of intercessory prayer: at the level of the spiritual self we are fully members one of another and the communion of saints is a real experience. In silent prayer my communion with the Father also brings me into communion with all life, and His Holy Spirit can effect communion with the personality of anyone I remember in prayer, whether or not I know him personally. As in so many other spiritual activities in this world, God acts only in collaboration with man, a measure of His courteous attitude to His creatures. When I remember someone in need in the deepest prayer, the Spirit will infuse that person — depending on his openness to help — and start a real process of healing. This real healing is not simply the removal of a troublesome complaint, be it physical, mental, or moral, but the renewal of the whole personality by the power of love. Healing is not to be thrust on the disordered person, as if by mental telepathy, but merely offered in love. To the one in need belongs the choice of accepting or rejecting the power of the Holy Spirit. Whatever the outward result of the prayer — whether the person improves or passes beyond death — there is a changed perspective on the part of the sufferer if he accepts the power of love. At last he begins to understand the role his own attitude has played in his mental and physical distress, and how essential a change of mind and heart (a metanoia) is for real healing to come about.

I often compare intercessory prayer with visiting a sick person in hospital. The good hospital visitor brings with him an inner radiance that lightens the darkness of the sick-bed and the clinical neutrality of the hospital ward. The good visitor sits quietly with the afflicted one, not engaging in an exhausting flow of conversation (which relates usually to the current problems of the visitor rather than to concern for the sick person), but simply flowing out in calmness and benediction to all around him. When he leaves the hospital, not only is his friend uplifted and blessed, but the whole atmosphere of the place is charged with hope and love. Even the other patients are blessed, and the staff's resources are renewed. If we could see intercessory prayer in the guise of visiting a distant person as an angel (or messenger) of light, we would come to realise that our presence is sufficient for the grace of God to descend on the afflicted one and renew his strength. We do not have to direct thoughts or pious attitudes towards him, but merely be with him in wordless communion.

Praying for Oneself

Personal petition is at the foot-hills of one's prayer life, but it should never be despised. The Lord's Prayer has several petitionary clauses. It is important, I believe, to understand that God does not alter His immutable law — be it material, psychical, or spiritual, it is one and the same law of God the Creator — to suit our own desires. But if we pray with ardour and perseverance, God will bring about such a change in our own consciousness and such an integration of our personality around the fixed centre, which is the spirit of the soul, that many things previously beyond our capacity may now become possible and attainable. The "miraculous" episodes described in the Bible, and especially in the life of Jesus, are, as I see it, largely factual. Admittedly some, especially those described in St. John's Gospel (which is a later work and one concerned more with the eternal meaning of the Incarnation and less with a day-to-day account of the ministry of Jesus), have overtones of parables rather than historical accounts, but the majority have the ring of immediate truth about them. I believe that such strong powers were the result of Jesus' direct attunement with His Father through the Holy Spirit. When a person attains this degree of integration, he moves in a vastly expanded realm of activity, and can understand life (and indeed have control over it) in a way that is hidden from the unawakened man. According to St. John, Jesus promised His disciples that they would perform even greater things than He had done (John 14:12). I believe this is how prayer works: if we ask in silence, the Holy Spirit will infuse us with new life, and we will become more fulfilled, spiritually conscious people. It is not that God does our work for us — this I am sure is contrary to divine law — but that He enables us to do the work more easily and efficiently, and with finer results.

If this is the case, it is evident that prayers for things are vain — and here I include wealth, success in an undertaking, and material prosperity. Even if these fortunes do befall us, there is no certainty that we will be better, more realised people as a result of them. On the contrary, material success unaccompanied by spiritual awareness and humility is more likely to harm the person and those dependent upon him than to give anyone prolonged happiness and contentment. But if we pray for forgiveness and the ability to forgive those whom we believe have wronged us, we will emerge stronger and less distracted by destructive thoughts of vengeance and crippling remorse for our own past selfish attitudes and actions. If we can become more patient and perseverant, our worldly affairs as well as our personal relationships will flourish, and our lives will become more productive. Thus prayers for qualities are of fundamental importance; through them we enter the Kingdom of God, directed there by His grace.

Nevertheless, as we grow in the life of prayer, such personal petitions fade into the background; all that concerns us is the beatific vision glimpsed in union with God, and the capacity to do His will more perfectly. All petition leads to the peak of the mountain of aspiration, where it is swallowed up in love and thanksgiving. Remember the greatest of all prayers, "O my Father, if it be possible, let this cup pass from me: nevertheless not as I will, but as thou wilt" (Matthew 26:39). This puts petition in its right perspective.

By all means ask for the smaller thing (for we are all small people, and even Christ was small when He became flesh for our sakes), but let us consecrate ourselves to the service of God at all times. This dedication will prevent us looking for results in prayer other than a slow transformation of our own personality.

Prayers for Cosmic Disorder

It is a hard thing for a rationalist to pray for a change in the weather or for the ending of some natural disaster. Indeed, I have stated that I do not believe God alters His law to suit us. Nevertheless, even the most scientifically orientated religionist will come spontaneously to pray to God for deliverance from drought, flood, or hurricane. When we are in dire straits, the reason submits gratefully to the higher intuition! And very often group prayer appears to be effective!

I believe that prayer in times of natural disaster is valid and most important. I suggested in a previous chapter that the weather and the cosmos itself may be more responsive to the human psyche and its disorders than is rationally tenable. I put forward a theory that natural disasters may be due to cumulative psychic influences emanating from disturbed people acting in large populations. If this is so — and admittedly we are in the realm of pure speculation here — could not prayer quieten the disturbed psyche of the mass of people, at last brought to their senses by the imminent peril that was confronting them all? The peace of God that passes all understanding, which the world cannot give, could at last still the minds of disordered people, and give the world a chance to function properly.

Whatever the explanation, I have no doubt about the propriety of such prayer. It may be the way of return of the agnostic to the divine threshold.

5

The Way of Action — Love and Service

SERVICE TO OTHERS is the one authentic way towards a knowledge of God. When we serve someone, we see him face to face, and as we lose ourselves in love for him, so God shows Himself to us in that person, whoever he may be, and in the relationship between ourself and the person. Neither the deepest meditation, nor the most ardent prayer, nor techniques for the development of the most profound self-knowledge pass beyond academic remoteness until they have been fertilised by service in the world.

The way of service is also the way of love. To serve with resentment or a cold heart is tantamount to cursing the person or institution one is assisting. We should not venture into service — and I speak here of spiritual service, and not the obligatory service we all have to perform in order to survive in the world — until we are prepared to give unstintingly of ourselves without counting the cost. Service expects no reward, looks for no approval or gratitude, and has no recompense other than seeing the other person happy and more complete in himself. This is the ideal of service; of course it cannot be followed all at once. Nevertheless, if we serve in humble, self-giving obedience, a radiance will in due course emanate from us to inflame the world.

Service does in fact benefit the aspirant directly by altering his attitude to life and broadening his sympathies for others. His sense of perspective is widened. A person in the throes of darkness and near despair following a severe personal disappointment or a tragic bereavement will eventually be released from his suffering by serving others. During the early stages of grief the person is usually paralysed emotionally, and can do very little other than remain alive; it is at this period particularly that the fellowship and prayers of friends can be of great help. But a time must come for a more positive approach to the world, and this is where the sacrament of service begins: it is making oneself available to other people in order that they may be released from suffering and inner imprisonment. The Holy Spirit is our guide and mentor in service. "The Spirit of the Lord God is upon me; because the Lord hath appointed me to preach good tidings unto the meek; he hath sent me to bind up the brokenhearted, to proclaim liberty to the captives, and the opening of the prison to them that are bound" (Isaiah 61:1). This is the meaning of service, and as one serves, so one is served by God to become a full person.

Life spent in the world is a continuous and arduous process of self-giving to the world. The world is assuredly our material for experimentation and self-expression, but it too has demands to make on us. We have to raise it from the corruption of mortality to the eternal life known to the children of God. We redeem the world by giving up ourselves to it, in following the way of Christ Who gave up His mortal life for the redemption of mankind. Thus the life of service is also the life of God made flesh. "Among you, whoever wants to be first must be the willing slave of all. For even the Son of Man did not come to be served but to serve, and to give up his life as a ransom for many" (Mark 10:43-45).

This is the way of love.

The Meaning of Love

God alone can define the depths of love. To us it is an attitude of mind that finds its expression in a way of life. It begins in the personal experience of losing oneself in the presence of another person, in whom one identifies one's noblest aspirations and deepest hopes. At first one sees the beloved as the embodiment of all that is finest in oneself, so easily are all thoughts projected on to him. But such an image of perfection is remote and static until a real, living relationship has commenced. It is now that the beloved steps down from his position of unearthly paragon to the solid earth with a body and mind of his own. To accommodate oneself to a self-governing person who does not, after all, conform entirely to one's own opinions, beliefs, and habits is the real test of love and the criterion of authentic service also.

Love proves itself in service; there is no more testing service than being close to another person through life's various vicissitudes. Such service is the heart of the all-important marriage relationship. It is one thing to live together with no ties other than mutual affection, so that the association can be broken at will as soon as one tires of it. It is something quite different to be willingly bound by a legal contract, so that one is obliged to go on with the relationship even when circumstances are difficult. But such a personal commitment in service is the way of mutual growth and understanding through the valleys and mountains of worldly life.

A very important stage in the growth of every person is the realisation that no outer circumstance of a material type can release him from his responsibilities. One has to proceed even in the darkness of life — including that of difficult relationship — before one's own defects are brought into the light of consciousness. To understand that our source of help lies within us — whence it proceeds from God — is the beginning of wisdom, and the life of service teaches us this great truth.

If we cannot face this truth, and terminate abruptly what is unpleasing to us, we cannot grow into a full person, or even lead a happy, successful life on a worldly level. We will drift from one unsuccessful relationship to another, always emerging wounded and resentful at our "bad luck" in forever encountering difficult, brutal, inconsiderate people, whether they be employers, working colleagues, or partners in marriage. How often have I met people who have never really made the grade! They are notorious among their own colleagues for their unpleasant personalities as well as their very modest professional ability, but they see nothing of this at all. Their lives are a dreary dirge of resentment and hatred of others whom they believe have betrayed them and robbed them of the success that was their due. They cast a malign psychic influence in their environment, and make everyone else unhappy also. It is from this morass of human inadequacy that political and racial hatred stems and bizarre religious cults and fanaticisms arise. These people have never known what true service means, and have regarded life as merely a means to their self-satisfaction and self-aggrandisement. The interesting thing is that not a few of them are ardent religionists, punctilious in outer orthodoxy (as were Jesus' opponents also). Bad religion (which is found in all the higher religions of the world) can be an impenetrable smoke-screen to conceal God and His searing truth from the sight of the believer.

If we persist in faith despite betrayal, disappointment, and disillusionment, we will be able, in the fullness of time, to transcend purely personal demands for happiness and fulfilment to gain an understanding of the wider issues of life. This is the fruit of service patiently carried out despite frustration and insult. We cannot know the reality of life while we continue to act as spoilt children for whom the world exists merely to amuse us. The bitterness of love is the reverse side of its sublimity; the arduousness of service is the source of unending joy in life.

If I really love someone, though my personal loyalty will not deviate from that person, my love will never remain attached to him exclusively; it will overflow to many people and become universal in sympathy. The type of affection that is restricted and exclusive does not deserve to be called love. It is really a physical and emotional attraction to some other person without whom life would scarcely be possible. Such egoistical possessiveness at best separates lover and beloved from wider participation in the world and so limits their growth into full persons. At worst it strangles the other in a web of jealous domination, so that it is a means of death. Indeed, devoted "love" of this restricted type often kills the second partner when the first has died, so meaningless is his life when bereft of the other. Real love, which follows long, arduous service, brings the person into deeper fellowship with many different types of people. It makes him less exclusive and more understanding. It breaks down denominational barriers, and brings people of different religious traditions into closer harmony.

This is the deeper meaning of tolerance. It is a real appreciation of the validity of another person's beliefs and way of life through the ability to identify oneself with him. There is no condescension in tolerance (as opposed to toleration, which is cold and has undertones of arrogance), but a lively participation in the views of other people so that one's own understanding can be enriched by them. And yet love in the form of tolerance does not annihilate the separate witness of any person or religious group. On the contrary, it draws into sharp relief all that is really vital and unique about the person and his tradition. If we could only speak of the various higher religious traditions in terms of their transcendent greatness, as witnessed by their mystics and saints (the two are often one), we would find a common denominator: the Christ within each one of us and the Holy Spirit that proceeds from Him. Then we would know the perfect love that casts out fear, a fear of personal annihilation into nothingness (which is the common view of physical death) or of incorporation into a system of belief in which the person ceases to exist (which is the end-result of atheistic collectivism). It can be seen that love is the way towards mystical union, a state of being in which the isolated self ceases to exist, but is raised to the spiritual statue of a real person in communion with all other selves in the love of God. This union is a gift of grace from the Word of God, and issues from God's love in the all-embracing fellowship of the Holy Spirit.

The Severity of Love

Love is warm and ardent, but it has on occasion also to be cold, even forbidding. The prophet Hosea speaks of God's love to Israel despite her frequent apostasies and gross idolatories. Hosea had understood the meaning of love through his own unhappy marriage with a prostitute. Despite frequent betrayals, he had never ceased to love his wife, for he was a man of love. This means that he was receptive to God's love, which is the source of the love we have one for another (1 John 4:10).

But the story of Israel was a sad one. Much suffering was illuminated by only scattered peaks of national triumph. This was not due to God's wrath, but to the inevitable results of violating God's law. If we choose anything other than the highest we know — and the children of Israel had that knowledge incontrovertibly fixed in the national consciousness from the time of their deliverance from Egyptian slavery — we fall from God's grace and suffer. The law is cold when it is disregarded and it brings suffering with it. This law is reflected in our lives today also. If we betray love, those around us will sever their fellowship with us, and we will be diminished. Likewise in any personal relationship, it is right to show displeasure when the other person acts selfishly and inconsiderately. It is by this almost automatic response that we can re-direct him on to the proper path. There may be times when a more severe degree of disapproval and remonstrance becomes necessary. This is a much more loving response than a mute acceptance of wrongful behaviour which can often signify a cold hostility or a deadly apathy. The law is clear: if we act anti-socially, we alienate ourselves from society, and deprive ourselves of the warmth of supporting love from our fellow men and from God. When the suffering that follows our selfish attitude to life has taught us our lesson we can be humble enough to confess our fault and receive forgiveness. This is the obvious way of self-understanding, and it is the duty of those who love the offender to treat him with the necessary severity until he comes to himself. But he should never be forsaken.

It is a strange paradox of the Bible that, while the fear of the Lord is the beginning of knowledge (Proverbs 1:7) and is indeed wisdom (Job 28:28), perfect love casts out fear (1 John 4:18). Both theses are profoundly true. We begin to fear God when we see, through a shaft of intuition, the scheme behind the marvellous array of natural phenomena that confront us all the days of our life. It is fear of self-destruction that keeps us obedient at least to the physical laws of the universe, while the bitter fruits of immoral and socially unacceptable behaviour teach us about the psychic and spiritual laws of God also. But as we grow into full persons, so our perspective is dominated less by considerations of survival and self-expression and more by a loving concern for humanity and the world we live in. It is at this juncture that we are prepared to give up our very lives for others; all personal clinging, which is the outer form of fear, is transcended by a self-giving love to the whole creation. This was the zenith of Jesus' life, and is repeated in the lives of even the humblest people who sacrifice themselves willingly for the good of their fellows.

The Forgiveness of Love

While it is important always to respond positively and decisively to a hostile or selfish action, there is a time when forgiveness and magnanimity should prevail over personal resentment and anger. To be aggrieved by injustice and seek redress is human; to respond to it in warmth and forgiveness is divine. But there is a spark of divinity in all of us, and at times even the most unlikely people may be inspired to act with a love and constraint that is supernatural in quality. When Jesus says, "Resist not evil; but whosoever shall smite thee on the right cheek, turn to him the other also... Love your enemies, bless them that curse you, do good to them that hate you, and pray for them which despitefully use you, and persecute you" (Matthew 5:39-44), He is giving a counsel of perfection. But perfection of this type is not visionary and impractical; it is the very way of authentic existence, and within the range of the aspiring person.

Such an attitude of joyous acceptance cannot be fashioned in our imagination by the thoughts of our minds. It comes to us as a special grace from God when we are ready to receive it. Prayer is the way for attaining the fitness necessary to receive God's grace; we should pray constantly that we may be able to forgive our enemies and turn their antipathy into love.

The occasion in any person's life when he can pass beyond the desire for retaliation and self-justification to an all-embracing love that asks no questions and makes no demands is the point in his existence when God has made Himself fully known to that person and is dwelling within him. Now at last the great injunctions of the Sermon on the Mount can be followed, not with the sense of overweening condescension that would be their effect in an unredeemed man trying to follow them by an act of will, but with overpowering love and blessing to the whole world. The explanation of this difference is of great importance. What we do of our own volition, be it ever so laudable, tends to inflate us and put us on a higher level than other people, whom we can only pity for their lack of understanding. The gratitude of the Pharisee that he is not as other men are is the typical result of such personal piety (Luke 18:9-14). Despite the performance of "good works", we are as unhealed in personality as ever. The service is self-centred and vain. But when God comes fully to us in grace following the prayer of self-abnegation, He cleanses our personalities and sets in motion the healing process; the inner proof of this healing is the awareness that we are forgiven and that we have nothing to be ashamed of or to hide from others.

It is interesting in this respect to note that, when Adam and Eve had turned from their state of natural union with all things to one of self-isolation through acquisitiveness, they were aware for the first time of their nakedness and tried to conceal it and themselves, even from God (Genesis 3:7-13). This marvellous parable shows us the result of withdrawing from God's grace. The reverse action, of humbling ourselves before Him and confessing our faults in faith, brings Him close to us once more. When we are cleansed of the results of our sinful actions, we have no need to project them on to other people, and can instead pour out the love that God has given us on to the world. At this stage we demand no justice for ourselves — and who could live if God gave us our just deserts!— but give of ourselves unstintingly as a living sacrifice for all creation.

I believe all mankind is destined to know this divine love. It is the impelling force for that service to God which is perfect freedom. The suffering servant described by Isaiah (53:1-12) typifies this higher love: by His scourging we are healed. The love of Jesus, that He took the burden of the psychic darkness of the whole world on Himself without complaint and with forgiveness (Luke 23:34), is a concrete manifestation of the highest service to which any man can aspire.

Contemplation and Action

To contrast the way of contemplation with that of action is to stress a very superficial dichotomy. Contemplation is the most exalted action a man can perform, for in it he comes as close to God as he can bear. But our life is not merely one of personal communion with God; it is also one of service to the world. Contemplation that does not find its expression in constructive worldly action is vain. On the other hand, worldly action, be it ever so well intentioned, becomes demonic if it is not moved by the love of God that comes to us in the self-giving of contemplative prayer. In theological terms faith precedes good works, but is always proved by good works. In the same way the grace of God precedes our own willed action, but the free will responds to grace by acting responsibly and charitably.

The work of everyday life is a marvellous illustration of collaboration between God and man. God will not act in the world unless we are prepared to play our part. But if we act without the impulse of God's grace, the results of our actions are thwarted and malign. It is the error of extreme forms of religious piety to see God as all powerful and man as a useless sinner. The final result of this view is quietism, an attitude which puts everything in God's hands and allows man no scope for action. The converse error is that of atheistic humanism, which sees man entirely responsible and in command of his own destiny depending on his innate powers. This is the prevailing view of many people nowadays, but man separated from the love and power of God is merely an intelligent animal whose works, though clever and impressive, tend to destruction rather than to life. Quietism leads to stagnation, both physical and moral, while atheistic humanism ends up in a denial of the fundamental human quality of spirituality, thus paving the way for degradation and destruction. It follows from this that the way of service should be initiated by contemplation and prayer, and fructified by worldly action.

In the story of Mary and Martha (Luke 10:38-42) there is a tendency amongst some people, wrongly conceived I believe, to suggest that Jesus exalts contemplation above service in the world. What he is really reproving in Martha is her tendency to magnify her labours at providing food and to claim special attention for herself on this account. If she had the still composure of her sister, she would be able to serve much more effectively and joyously, and see the Lord not only in His bodily form in her house but also spiritually in all the work of the household. No wonder Mary had chosen the better part, which was not to be taken from her.

In the seventeenth century a humble French soldier, nicholas Herman, entered a community of Carmelites in Paris in middle life, where he was called Brother Lawrence. This lowly man combined in his person the qualities of Mary and Martha. Even in the kitchen he was full of recollectedness and heavenly-mindedness. "The time of business" said he "does not with me differ from the time of prayer; and in the noise and clutter of my kitchen, while several persons are at the same time calling for different things, I possess God in as great tranquillity as if I were upon my knees at the Blessed Sacrament" (*The Practice of the Presence of God*, end of the fourth conversation).

Humble Brother Lawrence has surely much to tell us at present about the springs of real spirituality in a world of chaos. The little book mentioned above is as clear a guide to vibrant life as has ever been produced — outside the Gospel.

Conclusion

The basis of the way of service is that every task is done to the greater glory of God. This applies not only to human relationships, but also in our everyday work with inanimate objects and abstract ideas. The immaculate cleaning of a house, the considerate service that a shop assistant gives to the customer, the care we take of our clothes and possessions (which are in a very real way an extension of our own physical body), are all prayers of praise to God for His marvellous creation and thanksgiving that we are considered worthy enough to be custodians of the creatures of this world.

A meal prepared in love tastes quite different to one hastily put together without dedication to the task. One does not need great spiritual discernment to distinguish between a home of love and a house of disharmony. When one remembers a person with compassion, one is praying for him even if one is engaged in some outer action at the same time. When we give all our mind and strength to the work at hand, we are glorifying God and adding to His creation. To pray is an essential action of the spiritual life; to accept a sudden outside intrusion in our deepest prayers, so that we have to stop praying and pay attention to the source of the disturbance without resentment, is even more sublime. To give up our time to communion with God is excellent, but to expend ourselves fully in the loving service of our fellow men is an even more perfect way, for it is the way of prayer consummated in worldly service ("Inasmuch as ye have done it unto one of the least of these my brethren, ye have done it unto me" — Matthew 25:40).

6

The Sacramental Way

A SACRAMENT IS defined as an outward and visible sign of an inward and spiritual grace, and as such it is generally confined, in Christian usage, to a few liturgical acts, notably Baptism and the Holy Communion. But life itself is a sacrament; to him who is spiritually aware nothing ever happens that does not speak directly to him, revealing God's ever-present grace.

Through full participation in life's vicissitudes, we gain essential knowledge. Indeed, the quest for knowledge is a veritable obsession in contemporary society. People will travel large distances to hear alleged experts speak on spiritual matters. Yet the real source of wisdom is not to be found in the words of teachers, be they ever so enlightened, but in the apparently fortuitous events of our daily lives and in our response to them. The way of service that I have considered previously has at its end the discovery of the Holy Spirit active in all conditions of life. If we look for outer reward for service, we misunderstand the purpose of our work. But if we are prepared to give of ourselves unstintingly without seeking recompense or even personal recognition, we will be given an insight into the reality that underlies all work and sustains it at its core. At the same time, in dedicating ourself to the task at hand, we will lose our isolation in it to the glory of God, and will emerge, at least to some extent, as resurrected personalities in touch with eternal values.

Every action that is performed in full awareness, and suffused with joy and thanksgiving that we are the privileged ones to execute it, transcends its own temporal significance and partakes of something of the nature of eternity. It is raised from the evanescence of mortal things, here today and gone tomorrow, to take its place as an eternal witness to the presence of God in the form of human dedication and striving.

While God is assuredly not far from any of His creatures, be they living or inanimate, it is man's responsibility and privilege to evoke the divine quality in all the things of this world, and set in action the work of transfiguration. This collaboration between God and man in the world of form is the inner way in which all actions consecrated to the highest we know are sacramental.

The Eucharistic Sacrament

It would be presumptuous indeed to embark upon a theological discussion of the meaning and significance of the central sacrament of the Christian faith. We are here confronted by a mystery defying rational explanation, but one which is supernaturally illuminated by personal participation in the act of meditation and receiving the consecrated elements. It is indeed an "image" of Christ's death and passion, which too is so vast in conception and significance as to defy rational analysis and definition.

But one aspect at least is clear to me: the elements of our earth, bread and wine, when they are consecrated by one whose life is dedicated to the priestly office — itself a mystical state that lies outside both the purely human and the purely divine, yet acting as the mediator between the two — undergo a change in their spiritual nature. While never ceasing to be themselves as created things — bread and wine — they are no longer merely bread and wine, but are now exalted to their real function as a part of the body of Christ. Whatever is consecrated to God is no longer merely corruptible matter; it is matter redeemed and sanctified. Christ's body is the whole created universe dedicated to God in the selfless service of sacrifice. And the priest — who in the final phase will be Everyman — is not only the celebrant; he is also the victim who must be prepared to follow his Saviour even to death on the world's cross. Consecrated bread is the very body of Christ and the wine His blood, just as we who partake of them are His living body in the world. "The cup of blessing which we bless, is it not the communion of the blood of Christ? The bread which we break, is it not the communion of the body of Christ? For we being many are one bread, and one body: for we are all partakers of that one bread" (1 Corinthians 10:16-17).

As I have already said, whatever is consecrated to God's service in the love of Christ is redeemed, and it becomes holy. Yet it never ceases to be itself. There is no merging, or incorporation, of the creature into the Creator; there is rather a union, a union shown to the disciples during the mystery of the Transfiguration when Jesus was no longer a mere man but was revealed in the form of universal God — and yet never ceased to be fully Himself. God dwells in the depths, or core, of all His creatures — how could they exist without Him? But such a statement without qualification could tend towards a dangerous pantheism which simply identified God with the created, or natural order — and thereby obliterated the very being of God as creator and redeemer.

Another potential error is that of monism which sees God in all things, and nothing apart from God. Such an attitude, which is a hazard of emotionally based mystical experience, denies the unique identity of the creature or the obvious hierarchy of values that dominate the world of form. One of the greatest of the psalms, Psalm 139, sees God in hell as well as in heaven (verse 8), and in the darkness as well as the light (verse 12). Indeed, it is fortunate that He who is light and in whom there is no darkness at all (1 John 1:5), is the Master even of the dark things of the world. Otherwise there would be no hope for the world. However, for the divinity that is inherent in all things to be made manifest, the act of redemption, of consecration, by a dedicated humanity is mandatory. The relation between creature and creator is one of identity-in-difference. We are neither the same (the error of monism, kindly but confused) nor completely different (the error of dualism, which in its extreme gnostic forms sees the world of matter as the creation of the Devil and the "spiritual" world as the creation of God). The magnificent passage in St. Paul's letter to the Romans (8:21) about the deliverance of the creature from the bondage of mortality into the glorious liberty of the children of God, which I have more than once quoted, finds its promise in the act of self-dedication of man and his further consecration of all the world's creatures to God's service. This sacred duty finds it presage in the consecration of the elements of bread and wine in the Eucharist, which is indeed an outward and visible sign of an inward and spiritual grace. And in this service man himself grows a little into his divine nature, still, alas, hidden from most of us.

The Sacrament of Everyday Life

It would be wrong indeed to confine the sacramental way simply to liturgical practices. Rather are these religious sacraments to be regarded as guidelines to effective living in the world. Does not the communicant pray at the end of the Eucharist to be sent out into the world as a living sacrifice to God? If religious observance does not find its end in a transformed character and a new regard for the world, it is vain and merely deludes the religionist. Indeed, if the paraphernalia of religion has any justification at all, it is to put the person into closer communion with the unseen world of eternity. True religion is a way of approach to divine reality, whereas false religion usurps that reality and occludes the vision of God. This is the criterion of any new (or established) form of religion. Its claims may be enormous, but the acid test is always the same: do its members grow into the fullness of being shown to the world once and for all in the person of Jesus Christ? The religion that has grown up in the name of Christ is no more exempt from this judgment than those which do not recognise His supremacy. "Not every one that saith unto me, Lord, Lord, shall enter the kingdom of heaven; but he that doeth the will of my Father which is in heaven" (Matthew 7:21).

As we grow into the fullness of our personality, so we begin to divine the significance of every moment of our lives. The body and all the functions that appertain to it are no longer taken for granted and ignored; they are a source of blessing to us. We can say with the Psalmist, "I will praise thee: for I am fearfully and wonderfully made: marvellous are thy works; and that my soul knoweth right well" (Psalm 139:14). The functions of eating and excretion are now glorious in their own right, and the fact of health, whether bodily or mental, assumes its rightful place as a blessing from God.

Our work is no longer a burden, nor are we obsessed with considerations of its recompense or its importance in the scheme of things. It becomes instead an offering from ourselves to God the Creator, and its degree of perfection is a measure of our self-giving to Him. The works of our hands are in one respect evanescent: they are created with much effort but are destined to fall into oblivion as the sands of time cover up all mortal things. "As for man, his days are as grass: as a flower in the field, so he flourisheth. For the wind passeth over it, and it is gone: and the place thereof shall know it no more" (Psalm 103:15-16). There is no earthly thing that is assured an eternal abode, "for here have we no continuing city, but we seek one to come" (Hebrews 13:14). On the level of earthly sight man works in vain; the arguments in the Books of Job and Ecclesiastes confront this truth with stark realism.

But that which has been done well continues to exist both in the world of matter and in the reality of eternal life even after its external form has perished. A noble work, whether of art, science, or simple human compassion, raises the elements of the world from corruption to transfiguration. It reveals the divinity, the holiness, inherent in matter. It is, in fact, a secular counterpart of the consecration that is performed in the sacred office of the Eucharist. The world is never quite the same again after even the lowliest of its subjects performs even the simplest task in love and dedication. There is a subtle transformation in the elements of the earth which in turn finds its response in an altered psychic atmosphere around both the place of the work and the person of the labourer. Those coming into physical contact with the work, and also with the environment even after the outer form of the work has disappeared beneath the shifting sands of time, are renewed with hope and dedication. Holy places are easily discernible to those with psychic sensitivity, and their emanation infuses the weary heart with life and renews the disillusioned mind with hope and purpose.

We change the physical atmosphere of the world and the psychic environment of mankind by our works and the attitudes we evince in relation to the works. Life that is lived sacramentally — by which I mean in conscious awareness of the holiness of each event — transforms both the person and the world. It is our first presage of the resurrection of matter from the corruption of decay to the spiritual life of eternity. We cease to fear the future, instead accepting each challenge as a mile-stone in our own development. This acceptance is the outer sign of an inner trust in God's providence. Every new relationship, every change in the world's disposition, now becomes the material by which we grow more fully into the measure of a mature person. Far from trying to penetrate into the future by occult means and then changing it to suit ourselves, we advance joyfully into whatever is in store for us, trusting in the powers that God has given us and in His eternal presence with us. We make our future by our present actions; a full dedication of the person to the matter at hand — which is all he can control and be aware of — influences both the future and his attitude to it.

As a person becomes more aware of the sacramental quality of every action and occurrence in his life, so he may tend to be less devoted to overtly religious sacraments. The mature Quaker sees this sacramental quality particularly clearly and can dispense with all established religious sacraments, save, of course, the sacrament of silence which is the heart of Quaker worship. But there is no need for him to reject the Churches' other sacraments on this account; on the contrary, they can become even more sacred to a person whose religion is universal in scope and not restricted to any one form. On the other hand, there are some immature people who summarily reject the Churches' sacraments because they too affirm the sacramental nature of all life, but in their case this affirmation is clearly superficial and merely intellectual. In fact, their lives do not confirm their awareness of God in their daily affairs. The truth of God's presence in all things and all events is not intellectually deduced so much as inwardly experienced through the pain and suffering no less than the joy and exultation of a life dedicated to loving service.

To know of this presence of God in all things, and to make this knowledge real by an outflowing dedication in love to the world is the mark of a very advanced soul. Such a person will never reject any religious sacrament witnessing to the Living God, but will also be far above the restriction of a limited view of life that sees the sacraments only in a liturgical context.

The Sacrament of the Present Moment

In that classic of the spiritual life, *Self-Abandonment to Divine Providence* by the eighteenth-century French Jesuit Jean-Pierre de Caussade, special emphasis is laid on the sacrament of the present moment. God reveals Himself to the aware, dedicated aspirant in every moment of time. The statement, "Behold, I am making all things new" (Revelation 21:5), is no future promise but a factual account of the perpetual work of God on the open, dedicated personality during each moment of life. Every situation, every relationship brings us closer to the divine grace, if we are ready to receive it.

I have already spoken of the fallacy of trying to develop self-awareness by simply concentrating one's attention on one's own responses. The result of this technique of self-development is a truncation of that spontaneity which is the very essence of the joyous life. How can the Holy Spirit infuse His life-giving power into a self-conscious person intent only on analysis and control of himself and his environment? This selfish way isolates the person, and makes him remote from the world of relationships. Nevertheless, the practice of awareness is of great importance in the spiritual life; however, the awareness I commend is not that of the isolated self alone but of the moment at hand. This moment is the resultant of the outer flow of life and our response to it; both that which is outside us and our own personality play their part in this sacrament. There could be no present moment without the participation of the person himself, be he merely an observer. In this we see the sacramental nature of relationships. When the moment and all that belongs to it are accepted fully as an equal in love, the power of God reveals itself to me in that moment.

This is the essence of the I-Thou relationship, defined so wonderfully by Martin Buber. He says that all real living is meeting, and also, more challengingly, that by loving our neighbour we come to a unitive knowledge of God also. Indeed, though the divine essence is surely immanent in all creatures, and especially in its most conscious member, the human being, it is only through a self-giving relationship that God's hiddenness is fully manifest in our lives.

When we are able to give of ourselves fully to the moment in hand, the Holy Spirit can rule and direct our hearts; at this stage we can abandon ourselves joyously to divine providence. This does not mean that we become passive agents wafted to glory by the workings of God (the error of quietism). It means that the Holy Spirit marshals our inner resources by acting as the centre of integration in our life; the grace of God infuses our body, mind, and soul, so that all three at last work as they were destined to do: to the fulfilment of a proper person and to the glory of God. This is man's end, presaged in the person of Jesus Christ.

In the ascent to the sacrament of the present moment, all the disciplines I have already extolled — self-awareness, the way of suffering, meditation, prayer, and loving service — must first be given their full due. They are our way of progress from the torpor of apathetic self-delusion to the peak of heavenly vision. When the sacrament of the present moment extends to fill our whole life we have moved indeed from death to life, the unitive life in God.

Life as Sacrament

When life is lived sacramentally, in conscious awareness of the holiness of each moment, many blessings accrue. The great injunctions of the Sermon on the Mount about living fully in the present and not losing ourselves in fruitless speculations about the future become the obvious way to abundance in all things (Matthew 6:19-34). This is no invitation to improvidence, such as the Prodigal Son's selfish folly engendered with its all too predictable results; it is full awareness of and participation in the present, which alone, as I have already pointed out, controls our response to the future. Assuredly no

one has a perfect knowledge of what is to be — even Jesus
denied absolute knowledge of this type (Mark 13:32) — but if
we are calm and self-possessed, we will be able, with God's
help, to adapt ourselves remarkably effectively even to the
worst calamities that may befall us. We all have, praise be to
God, to cast off our physical body in death at some time. The
man who lives in the present is never far away from the
awareness of death, but this is no morbid preoccupation. It is
instead a joyous expectation, and all his actions are directed to
leaving behind him as perfect a piece of work and as little
disorder as possible before he commences the new round of his
existence.

He who fears death also fears life. He who loves life and all
the creatures of life has already passed from death to the life of
eternity.

When we live sacramentally, we are less concerned about
what the future has in store for us, and our actions are not
directed primarily towards results. Instead we do the work for
its own sake and to its own glory (and the glory of God), and
do not become trapped in vain imaginings or dashed hopes. We
can begin to see the strength of St. Paul's dictum, "We know
that all things work together for good to them that love God"
(Romans 8:28). While we naturally hope for success, we are
more inclined to leave the means of success and its fruit to
God, and make fewer demands ourselves. For what is success
and what is failure? What appears to be initially successful may
have unforeseen results of a disastrous type; what started as a
disaster may be later consummated in triumph. The disaster of
Jesus' crucifixion preceded the downflow of the Holy Spirit on
His disciples and the birth of the Christian Church.

All these considerations lead to the right understanding of
positive thinking. Its power is correctly stressed by various
contemporary schools of metaphysical training, but often its
use is directed to selfish ends or to a philosophy totally
divorced from reality. We think positively when we are able to
confront the future with calm confidence and a sense of
adventure, not denying the difficulties and dangers ahead, but
fixed in our faith that all will be well, and indeed is well in the
realm of eternal life. "The righteous man will live by his

faithfulness" (Habakkuk 2:4, re-echoed in Romans 1:17). By constructive thinking, we are not irreparably crushed by the rebuffs of fortune or the unexpected frustration of our dearest hopes. Positive thinking leads to that state of equanimity in which we can take both our failures and successes in their stride without being emotionally disturbed, and simply get on with the task at hand.

This is the "holy indifference" taught by Christian mystics. It is not a condition of apathy; on the contrary, it is one of radiant joy in the participation of life and all it offers one each moment in time.

I might add here in parenthesis how powerful negative thinking can be, especially to those, like myself, of great psychic sensitivity. I have only to be in the company of people who see the worst side of every situation, who cannot imagine any purpose or meaning in life, and who cavil and carp at every constructive thought, to be reduced very rapidly to a state of darkness and creative impotence. Fortunately I have learned to counter this baneful depression by escaping from such people as soon as possible, going into a quiet place, and praying silently to God. His divine grace soon inspires me with a fresh vision of wholeness. I can recommend this spiritual exercise to anyone who is depressed because of some outer disappoint-ment; it is a far more effective therapy than burdening those around one with one's emotional problems. By this I do not suggest that we should not all bear each other's burdens, but there comes a time in one's own travail, which is really a mile-stone on one's journey to full humanity, when, having confided one's difficulty to those close to oneself, one should be quiet and let their prayers as well as one's own set in action the resources that come to one from God. The constant discussion of one's trouble, especially if it is a physical malady, accentuates its power, and if there is idle chatter about it amongst one's various acquaintances, it can acquire a psychic as well as a physical stranglehold.

The Sacramental Nature of Relationships

We do not live alone; all life is consummated in a relationship with the other. This other is personal, whether its form is human, animal, vegetable, or mineral. In the Buddhist tradition the existence of an independent, or private, centre of consciousness is denied. This doctrine of "anatta" (literally no soul) is superficially absurd, for the discovery of an inner centre of awareness, the personal self, is a part of the way to becoming a full person. But, in fact, it is merely the reflection of the spiritual self in the tarnished mirror of worldly life. And the spiritual self is never private and self-enclosed. As we have previously noted, it is in psychic communion with the totality of the universe, and through its spirit even with God Himself. I am a full person only when I have ceased to be isolated. I am fully myself when I am in relationship with the other. This is the I-Thou relationship I have already mentioned, as defined by Buber. The statement of Jesus that "where two or three are gathered together in my name, there am I in the midst of them" (Matthew 18:20) is an inevitable truth. When we are met together in the name (or nature) of Christ, which is love, He cannot but be with us.

It follows from this that every relationship is sacred. This applies especially to the most intimate of all relationships, the sexual one. It is a sacrament, and is defiled to the detriment of all participating in it. It is worth remembering that in the properly consummated sexual act, an act in which both parties have lost themselves in love for each other, each experiences a new reality, one that transcends the narrow isolation of personal gratification. Such an experience is the glimpse of mystical union destined for Everyman — by which I mean the person who does not aspire to great spiritual understanding but lives in a useful mundane way — by God's grace. I believe that this is the primary purpose of sexual union; the other two, growth into a full person and the procreation of the race, are secondary to it. It follows from this that sexual intercourse is a holy action, and should not be contemplated except in a spirit of awe and gratitude. How far man has fallen from this understanding is a measure of his distance from the divine nature implanted in him. I should add at the same time, that those exceptional people called to the state of celibacy in the cause of a greater love for all mankind, may also experience mystical union in their unceasing self-giving to others.

Nor does the sacredness of relationships end at the human level. We cannot abuse an animal, plant, or even the physical part of our environment without diminishing both the world and ourselves. To be sure, we cannot exist in our fleshy form except by preying on the "lower" forms of life and on the earth itself. All that is worldly is mortal. Man himself is not destined to a prolonged existence in the form of a physical body. But whatever we use in the inevitable I-It relationship must be treated with the greatest reverence, so that its integrity, in the form of eternal truth, may be acknowledged even when its physical form is sacrificed to sustain us. Man's unique position lies in being at one and the same time a part of the world's creatures and also separate from them. In the Genesis story God gives man dominion over every living thing that moves upon earth and over every herb (Genesis 1:28-30). The resolution of the paradox of identity and separation lies in the Christhood that is the promise in store for us all. In a supreme relationship we are to give up ourselves for the world, even as Jesus did for mankind. And the result will be that both man and the world will pass from corruption to the eternity of spiritual reality.

7

Warnings on the Way

ONE LIGHT SHINES through the whole path to authentic life, the light of God, Who is present in every activity to which we give ourselves body and soul. God does not have to be sought out in far-away places, nor is He the preserve of the intellectually competent, nor have occult techniques to be mastered before He can be found. He is closer to us than our own soul; indeed, He makes Himself known to us on the path to self-knowledge. He is the boon companion of the child, while obscure to the intellectually inflated adult. No wonder Jesus taught that unless we become as little children we shall never enter the kingdom of heaven (Matthew 18:3). And yet St. Paul, in an equally famous passage, speaks of the necessity of putting away childish things when we grow up into full adulthood (1 Corinthians 13:11). It is evident that knowledge is a vital part of spiritual progress, and yet can all too easily obscure the vision of God.

In the Hindu tradition the mind is described as the slayer of the real; a brief sojourn among the usual run of academicians and applied scientists, in whose company all imaginative thought is rapidly silenced, will soon convince the outsider of this truth.

The Way of Knowledge and its Pitfalls

There are two types of knowledge. The first is the common one that separates the knower from the known, which becomes an object to be mastered and controlled. This is the I-It relationship of Buber, and is the type of knowledge the world demands and esteems. To be sure, man has attained his position of supremacy by virtue of it. In the most positive way he has, through the rapid advances of scientific knowledge, dominion over all the outer aspects of the world, so much so that he is now poised on the knife-edge of destruction not only of the earth but also of himself.

The second type of knowledge brings both knower and known into a creative relationship in which the transcendent reality underlying it is revealed. This is the unitive knowledge whose nature is love. It is the stuff of life as well as its meaning, and is the I-Thou relationship. It leads us directly to a knowledge of God, for it is above all sacramental. This unitive type of knowledge is clearly holy, and is the destination of the spiritual path. But is separative knowledge also of use spiritually, or is it always perverse?

This question deserves a firm answer. All knowledge is potentially beneficial provided it is not the end of the quest. In the spiritual path a detailed understanding of the body, mind, and soul, as far as this is possible, is most important. It is a basic truth that dietary excesses and alcoholic intemperance damage the body and weaken the mind. A person on the spiritual path learns almost intuitively to cut down on his food intake and to take as little alcohol (and the various psychotropic drugs that are so widely prescribed for sleeplessness, anxiety, and depression) as possible. The vegetarian way becomes ever more attractive — though the aspirant will never embarrass his host by indulging his personal whims regarding food — and smoking loses its emotional urgency.

Likewise the mind can be stilled and kept relaxed by the practice of meditation. An attitude of benediction towards all living things is a wonderful way of attaining meditative calm during the working hours. The Buddhist ideal of "meditation in action" is an application of the inner stillness attained during silent meditation to the world around one during the heavy business of our waking hours. As I have already stated, the technique of meditation and the practice of prayer have to be with us at all times and places if they are to be real.

The most detailed scheme of spiritual knowledge in

existence is the Indian system of Yoga, which finds its culmination in the Yoga Sutras of Patanjali. As is well known to practitioners of this system, there is no part of the personality that is excluded from its comprehensive surveillance. The bodily movements and breathing exercises are the most celebrated parts of the system, and each movement is performed with that complete awareness and self-dedication which is the true meaning of meditation. In this way the sacrament of the body is realised. And yet this part of Yoga is at the foot-hills of the real quest, the consecration of the person to God, however He may be conceived (and here the undogmatic Hindu-Buddhist approach to ultimate reality can be much more liberating than the fixed dogmatism of Western theistic religion which all too often has parcelled the Deity into tidy categories of thought). The psychic constitution of the personality, a branch of knowledge still obscure to Western psychology, has from time immemorial been symbolised in the Yogic tradition in the concept of subtle immaterial bodies interpenetrating the material physical body and having well-defined centres of psychic sensitivity which are called "chakras". To those who are psychically aware this scheme is accurate enough, even if its conceptual formulation is inadequate and obtuse. I personally was aware of the centres through my own experience long before I read books on Hindu metaphysics. It is incidentally to the credit of the Theosophical Society and its various offshoots that this knowledge has been transmitted to the West, albeit in a rather debased, sensationalised form. In fact, the deeper contemplative tradition of the Catholic Church, both Eastern and Western, has long been aware of the psychic centres also, although it has laid less emphasis on them. The Orthodox Church's celebrated Jesus prayer is also called the prayer of the heart: it is the intention of the disciple to bring his mind (from the head) into proximity with his heart (the centre of love and compassion). Though all the centres are important, it is unwise to meditate on the higher ones until the heart is fully active. Then at least one's endeavours will be consummated in love rather than in self-seeking.

It is evident that techniques can be of great value in fostering the spiritual life. They can unfortunately equally easily be the means whereby the isolated self is glorified and the vision of God banished. It is often this undesirable element which dominates the lives of technical practitioners. Their endeavours open to their vision vast expanses of psychic territory, including in some instances possible glimpses of past lives, and they become increasingly inflated and arrogant. This is where spirituality degenerates into frank occultism. It is probable that a considerable amount of psychical information derived from occult techniques has some basis of truth, and yet in itself it leads nowhere. Moreover, it does have the baneful effect of diverting the aspirant from communion with God into self-limiting psychical experiences whose ultimate path is a dead-end.

Many people of the West have discarded the religious tradition of their particular culture, be it Jewish or Christian. But not a few have discovered the insufficiency of a humanistic ethic that denies the inner spiritual dimension of life. These people have moved in considerable numbers into the realms of occult speculation and practice using meditation techniques derived from Eastern sources that by-pass the rational mind and the sphere of moral values. As a result they speak glibly about spiritual things and indulge in vain metaphysical speculations, but they remain painfully undeveloped as persons. Nor will they ever develop in this life-time until they dedicate themselves to the greater themes of universal religion: the building of the person, the transfiguration and resurrection of the world, and the salvation of the created universe. These themes cannot be approached by psychism, but only by true religion.

One can deduce from this that techniques for developing the inner life are as likely to cause harm as good, unless the person is dedicated to the quest for God before he begins. And this dedication is no theoretical attitude; it is shown by self-giving service in the world in whatever situation the aspirant finds himself. The dedicated person will never be alone. He will find someone further on the path to help him. Such is the spiritual director or the guru. "When the pupil is ready, the master appears". He is not to be obsessively sought; if one is doing the right work, the Holy Spirit will direct one to him. He is known by his unobtrusive modesty, his sanctity, and his outflowing love. And he is merely the way-shower. When his function is completed, he retires into the shadows, and his pupil now assumes his mantle. The story of the translation of Elijah and the falling of his mantle on to Elisha typifies the master-pupil relationship (2 Kings 2:1-14).

Knowledge leads us from faith to a scientific understanding of the world around us. The highest knowledge informs us of the impossibility of ever comprehending the world, or even ourselves, by the use of the naked intellect, or reason. It is then that wisdom begins; this is knowledge fertilised by awe in face of the mystery of creation. And this awe is consummated in a way of knowing that is no longer restricted to rational categories of thought, but transcends the reason without denying it. This is the non-rational approach to reality. I repeat, it does not contradict reason — if so it would be irrational and demonic — but it extends our reason through understanding gained from reaches of the mind that are far beyond consecutive thought. The psychical and spiritual realms are finally opened to us, and they inform us of relationships that lie beyond anything that the reason can penetrate.

The final relationship is love — a complete self-giving to the totality of existence. This is unitive knowledge, and it proceeds from God Who transcends all relationships and in Whom all relationships are held together. The coincidence of love and wisdom is the highest category that the human mind can conceive. It is a union of the head and the heart, and is the nearest man can approach to the divine mystery.

The Way of Spiritual Gifts and their Danger

I have already noted that, as a person progresses on the path to divine knowledge, so various psychic gifts may be bestowed on him. This is as it should be. The spiritual law is, "Seek ye first the kingdom of God, and His righteousness; and all these things shall be added unto you" (Matthew 6:33). Gifts bestowed on an aspiring person are a proof of God's grace. They are beacons of encouragement to the aspirant, and a blessing to the world around him, because he uses these gifts with self-effacement and wisdom. He has no need for personal power inasmuch as he is in receipt of divine power, a power which the servant uses to raise the fallen creatures around him. The gifts of the Spirit are defined in detail by St. Paul in 1 Corinthians 12: wise speech (wisdom), putting the deepest knowledge into words, faith of an unusually intense degree, healing gifts, miraculous powers, prophecy, distinguishing true spirits from false (the discernment of spirits), ecstatic utterance (tongues), and the ability to interpret that utterance.

Now most of these gifts are psychic in nature, and can be demonstrated by people who are not necessarily dedicated to the spiritual path; this applies particularly to some of the healing gifts and some aspects of "miraculous" powers. Some gifts may occur at an early stage of spiritual awakening — this applies particularly to tongues of ecstatic utterance and their interpretation. Others, like the gifts of wisdom, knowledge, and prophecy, occur at a more advanced level and are particularly to be esteemed. Though every gift is of the Holy Spirit, St. Paul makes it clear that spectacular utterances of ecstasy are amongst the least exalted inasmuch as they are essentially private testimonies unless they can be reliably interpreted by someone else (1 Corinthians 14: 1-19).

Psychic gifts are the hall-mark of the Charismatic Movement which is sweeping through most of the main Christian denominations at present. This pentecostal renewal is generally to be welcomed, for it has, as I said already, put new life into the rather staid, unimaginative worship of the church. Its keynote is joy, which is rare amongst conventional churchgoers. It has led to a greater sense of community and more love amongst its members. But its danger is obvious. It tends to exalt those who believe they have been baptised into the Spirit, and gives them an aura of superiority. The divisive nature of the Charismatic Movement is notorious; whole congregations have been split asunder by it. And yet it is also breaking down denominational barriers and effecting an ecumenism that only the Holy Spirit can give (Ephesians 4:3). In this dichotomy we can see both the dangers of spiritual gifts in immature individuals and their larger benefits in the hands of loving people.

The danger of any gift of the Spirit is that it inflates the personality of the recipient without integrating it. This applies no less strongly to the psychic powers inherent in Spiritualism than to the spiritual gifts of Pentecostalism. It is interesting that the Pentecostalist deprecates Spiritualism, asserting that all alleged powers deriving from the psychic realm are of demonic origin. On the other hand, he believes his own gifts are from the Holy Spirit and therefore impeccable in quality. The convinced Spiritualist, on the other hand, attributes his powers to exalted "guides" on the other side of life, whom he tends to magnify almost to divine eminence. The one feature these diametrically opposed views have in common is a conviction of their own infallibility. The source, whether it be the Holy Spirit Himself or a great spirit "guide," has the whole answer. The danger of arrogance, intolerance, and above all superstition and ignorance is very great.

There is a deep longing in most of us for some source above ourselves, whether we call it God or some supernatural entity, that will guide us and make our work prosper. I personally believe that all gifts come from the Holy Spirit, and are therefore charismatic, but that they often infuse highly fallible men who then colour the gift with their own personality. It follows therefore that until the personality is becoming integrated around the centre of the soul where God is known, any gifts that may be made manifest in that person will tend to exalt him above his fellows. This is called psychic inflation: it is of almost universal prevalence amongst practitioners of Spiritualism, and it leads to disaster when the "guide" in due course fails. In the instance of the undeveloped Spiritualist and Pentecostalist, the exaltation of the personality can move beyond mere psychic inflation to spiritual pride, the deadliest of all sins. Such a person looks down on others (for he alone "knows"), judges and condemns all and sundry, and is generally so enamoured with himself and his gifts that he begins quite unwittingly to identify himself with God.

Apart from the personal hazards of psychic inflation and spiritual pride, abused spiritual gifts weaken the power of judgment, inasmuch as they are given undue precedence over the rational side of the personality. They also override the freedom of the awakened will. It is a painful fact of life that our difficulties are overcome by slow, arduous toil using every part of the personality. There is no magic way of release, only a path of hope through sacrifice: Jesus said, "Come unto me, all ye that labour and are heavy laden, and I will give you rest. Take my yoke upon you, and learn of me; for I am meek and lowly in heart; and ye shall find rest unto your souls. For my yoke is easy, and my burden is light" (Matthew 11:28-30). He promises relief through the abundant life He came to show us, but He does not offer magic solutions. The problem is solved by the divine-human collaboration, not by God's miraculous intervention.

All this is particularly pertinent to the healing gifts of the Spirit. There is no real healing that comes by a dramatic psychic gesture, whether it is effected by a Spiritualist or a Pentecostalist. True healing infuses the whole of the person; it cannot by-pass the body and its natural functions, nor can it disregard the mind, or psyche. In other words, all healing has a medical and psychological component, which in man's present state of evolution is pre-eminent. This is assuredly not the whole of healing, but it is at least the beginning of the process. The more experienced charismatic healer usually acknowledges the importance of the medical practitioner and psychotherapist, and tries to work in collaboration with them. This is where the Church's Ministry of Healing could be so useful in providing a respected forum in which the scientist and the charismatic could work together. At present the scientist tends to regard the charismatic healer with a mixture of suspicion and contempt due to an unacknowledged hostility towards and fear of anything that threatens his limited view of reality. The Spiritualist and the Pentecostalist are often so full of their own knowledge (transmitted, in the case of the Spiritualist, by his "guide") that they have little time for any other point of view. Until the various insights of all the agencies of healing are regarded with dispassionate respect, the full range of salvation will remain unexplored. At present each agent is isolated in his own conceptual framework.

To sum up, let us exalt the fruits of the Spirit: love, joy, peace, longsuffering, gentleness, goodness, faithfulness, meekness, and temperance (Galatians 5:22). These are the proof of the Holy Spirit at work within the personality. It would be surprising if, as a result of the integration of the personality thus achieved, there was not a concomitant intellectual and psychic unfolding which manifested itself in the well-defined gifts of the Spirit. The least of these is the emotional release effected by non-rational prayer in tongues; the finest is the intellectual and spiritual synthesis made real in prophecy. But the greatest gifts of the Spirit are the ones attributed prophetically to the Messiah: wisdom, understanding, counsel, power, knowledge, and fear of the Lord (Isaiah 11:2). To these piety is added in the Christian tradition. These seven gifts humble the person before the face of God. Then he is able to use the psychic gifts of the Spirit with impunity.

Authority and the Danger of Subjectivity

The nature of authority in the spiritual life is a fundamental question. All aspirants on the path would affirm that God alone was the authority whom they served and trusted — no matter how they conceived Him. But no man has ever seen God; at the most we are given glimpses of His nature. As the Bible says, the wonders of the physical universe testify to the glory of God, and yet these are but the fringe of His power; how faint is the whisper that we hear of Him, for who could fathom the thunder of His might? (Job 26:14).

There is no one infallible seat of authority below the heavenly throne, but in order of priority I would place the inner light of man (the spark of God placed deep within the soul) and the wisdom of the human race. This wisdom is compounded of three elements: a scriptural authority, an ecclesiastical tradition, and the fruits of reason that have accrued from the intellectual, artistic, and scientific achievements of past generations of men. In the end we have to obey the dictates of our own conscience, for God is eternally making all things new (Revelation 21:5). Every life is a mile-stone in the progress of the whole human race on the path to self-mastery and consecration of itself to God's service. We cannot turn back or find refuge in old formulae. This would be a real betrayal of the work of the Holy Spirit, Who, contrary to the belief of some Christians, did not end His work after the apostolic period, but is as active in the lives of men today as He was in those far-distant times. And His activity is primarily that of leading us into all truth. Whatever is of durable value in the scriptures, the tradition of the Church, or the later achievements of mankind has been directly inspired by the Holy Spirit. He has no favourites, but works indiscriminately amongst all those who are prepared to give up their lives to the service of the highest they can conceive; this may be scientific truth, aesthetic beauty, or self-transcending love. In this true aristocracy, the caste-mark is self-dedication to the highest that can be known through the reason. Where truth, beauty, and goodness coincide, there God will be recognised by the intellect. But He is never known intellectually. Unitive knowledge is supernatural; God gives Himself to those that know their need of Him (the poor in spirit), and the proof of this grace is the changed person who has received it.

This means that the person who gives of himself fully to life will reach a point where his personal intellectual endeavours will be overshadowed by something external to him. This is the cloud of unknowing. It will take him up into itself, and he will see that which is hidden from mortal sight, and comprehend that which lies beyond rational understanding. Then he will know the truth, the truth that sets him free (John 8:32). It is noteworthy that Jesus was recognised by the common people around Him to speak with a note of authority that was denied the doctors of the law (Mark 1:22). Their authority was scriptural and traditional — in itself unexceptionable — but it was not confirmed in their hearts. One begins to know and to speak with that inner authority when one's personality is cleansed in the refining fire of God's love, which comes, as I have already stated, to those who are giving themselves unstintingly to the world around them.

But how does the authentic inner voice of God differ from the merely subjective sensation of certitude to which we are all heir? This certitude may vary from a "hunch" about some future event — which may or may not be confirmed — to the expression of some deep inner prejudice of which we are scarcely aware. The most important difference between inner authority and subjectivity is that true authority does not boost, or inflate, one's personality. On the contrary, the person endued with true authority not only recognises his own unimportance in the scheme of things but is indeed oblivious of himself in his devotion to the Most High. Nor is he personally affronted by opposition or derision. On the other hand, subjectivity tends to exalt the person, making him feel rather special and, like the Pharisee in the famous parable, decidedly unlike other men (Luke 18:11).

The inner voice does not claim an authority that disregards or dispenses with the external sources of authority which guide men's lives: scripture, tradition, and reason. On the other hand, the fresh insights it affords illuminate these other sources of authority and bring them into clearer perspective. Jesus said, "think not that I am come to destroy the law, or the prophets; I am not come to destroy, but to fulfil" (Matthew 5:17). Subjectivity has little time for sources of authority outside itself; it rightly sees in traditional wisdom a mortal enemy to be discountenanced at all costs. The most dangerous type of subjectivity is sectarian religious enthusiasm — the word itself literally means a state of possession by a god. The god that possesses the sectarian enthusiast is some doctrinal formulation, or a striking idea, or a psychic gift, but it is not the one God in whom we live, and move, and have our being. The sectarian enthusiast jettisons the painfully acquired authority of reason, often discarding precepts that have stood the test of time, simply because it conflicts with his private system of belief. He interprets scripture idiosyncratically, and fiercely attacks any church discipline outside his own revelation. Above all, he is devoid of love for people, but is devoted exclusively to his beliefs.

Subjectivity isolates the person progressively from his fellow men. They begin to feel uneasy in his presence, and are aware of his disturbed emotional state. The authority of the inner voice may be profoundly disturbing — as was the message of Jesus and the Prophets of Israel — but it is also invigorating and life-enhancing. It leads to profound self-searching, and the person emerges from its grim scrutiny cleaner and purer than before.

Subjectivity is personal, and proceeds by the assertiveness of the personal self. It is loud, assertive, and anxious for power over others. It seeks to justify itself. The authority from on high transcends personality, for it proceeds from the spirit of the soul. It is quiet, peaceful, and makes no attempt either to coerce others or to exalt itself. This is because it arises from God, Who is the source of all power. Far from imposing itself on others, it remains calm and at rest. It is, in fact, actively sought by those who understand reality. It does not lead the searcher into material prosperity, but it does show him the way to the abundant life.

There is a centre in us where truth can be discerned. It is the pearl of great price for which everything else we possess has to be sacrificed (Matthew 13:46). Our whole life should be dedicated to this greatest of all quests; its destination as well as its prime mover is God Himself. The external authorities of scripture, tradition, and reason are constant beacons on the path of self-discovery, which are disregarded at our peril. But in themselves they cannot take us to the throne of the heavenly grace; they are merely way-showers. If we rely on any of them without the illumination that proceeds from the inner light of the awakened soul, they will simply imprison us in limited modes of thought. The biblical fundamentalist interprets the scriptures according to the outdated thoughts of a primitive religious culture. The traditionalist hides beneath past forms to escape from the challenge of the Holy Spirit in his life. The rationalist will not quit the incarcerating palace of intellectual certitude to enter fresh fields of speculation and endeavour. Neither the fundamentalist, nor the traditionalist, nor the rationalist can escape from the imprisoning bonds of his particular conceptual system. This is the danger of obsessive objectivity, the enslavement of the person to an external source of authority.

The danger of subjectivity is that of overweening personal pride and a reliance of an inner "revelation" that may be delusive in quality and dictatorial in power. There are three sources of inner revelation: the unconscious part of the psyche (which is the commonest source, and often projects itself into consciousness in the form of an outer directive to action), psychic communication from an outside source, whether alive in the flesh or in the world beyond mortal death, and finally the voice of God. The last is obviously desirable, but the first two, though not to be discountenanced outright, are clearly of indeterminate nature. If one has the inner discernment to analyse the psychological and psychic components of subjective revelations, one can separate from them what is really beneficial. Thus the revelations that follow vivid dreams, which I have already discussed, are, in the great majority of instances, psychologically mediated, and can be very useful pointers to our unconscious attitudes. But they must be subordinate to the conscious mind, which can then analyse them. Psychic communication can on occasions be very beneficial and give us an indication of aspects of life beyond rational understanding. But once again it must be under the supervision of the conscious mind which should, through discernment, accept or reject the revelation according to its intrinsic merit.

Spiritual revelation never claims supremacy over the conscious mind. It is, by its very nature, supreme and the reason bows in reverence before it. It does not give us personal instruction or information, nor is it concerned about our individual well-being, material success, or prosperity, nor does it direct us into the most rewarding path. But it does infuse the whole personality with warmth, it integrates the personality around the "centre" of the soul (or the spirit), and it allows the person himself to decide his future in a mature, responsible way. It guides us by making us complete people; it does not dictate to us, and then leave us as incomplete and inadequate as before. In fact, the authority from the light of God transcends both the categories of subjectivity and objectivity. It is transpersonal, and its action is directed towards the fulfilment of true humanity in all mankind. It comes quite unobtrusively to many people at various times and in diverse ways as a sudden widening of spiritual vision, so that what was previously obscure in the scriptures, or confusing in the past course of their own lives, now takes on a new light and is illuminated with meaning.

One baneful defect victims of both extreme subjectivity and objectivity share is an obsessional fear that the basis of their belief will be shattered. When the Spiritualist's "guide" is disproved, or modern biblical criticism demolishes a fundamentalistic belief in the scriptures, or psychical research causes a materialistic view of life to founder, their various protagonists will fight bitterly against the inroads of disbelief. The results are no credit either to religious truth or scientific objectivity. Indeed, there is much subjectivity in even the most objective views of reality! On the other hand, the person who speaks with an inner authority that is divine in origin takes little thought for himself. He has moved beyond the point of coincidence of contradictory facts, and realises their resolution, not by emotion or intellect, but by a sense of humour that sees the absurdity of all dogmatic statements in a world that is beyond rational understanding. A sense of humour is an important quality of the mystic whatever his religious belief. It is seen in the intuitive solution of nonsensical riddles (koans) in the Zen Buddhist tradition, in the quaint and beautiful legends of the Hasidic rabbis of the eighteenth century, in the lives of St. Francis and St. Teresa, and in not a few of the retorts of Jesus — often taken with such straight faces by those who read the Gospel dutifully but unimaginatively.

Where there is an ebullient sense of humour, the Holy Spirit cannot be far away.

A Parable

There was a man whose life was dedicated to understanding the secrets of existence. He wanted to know the ultimate meaning of life. So he spent his time reading learned treatises on comparative religion. As these took him only a limited way, he dipped further into sources of occult lore, and consulted many men who were experts in this field. His desire to master the secret of life was overwhelming, and so he put himself into the hands of a master of the way. The master said, "Put your hands into this pair of gloves, and I will direct them to the very threshold of Deity."

And so the aspirant's hands were ensheathed in the gloves, and he was assuredly taken on a celestial journey. During its course the whole psychic world was revealed to him, the future was laid open, and also his past lives. Indeed, he knew everything there was to know about his origin and destiny. Eventually he felt the distinct impact of God Himself. Through his gloves he could sense the divine essence, and be aware of the very blueprint of creation. And yet he could never know God as the simplest mystic knew Him. How strange it was that he, a man who had been schooled in the most intricate occult techniques and had the whole of heaven in his head, was further from a knowledge of God than the unlettered people he had read about, who through no apparent merit of their own, had been given the impress of God's mighty love.

He tried harder and harder to come to know God, read more books, and went to other masters who taught him many more techniques. But they seemed to separate him from God and imprison him in an edifice of metaphysical speculation.

At last the time came for him to die, full of unimportant knowledge but as far from the divine wisdom as the most vapid hedonist or the most bigoted religionist. After he passed over into the life beyond death, he was confronted by a Master of real wisdom. He asked him why he had failed in his quest despite his intensive endeavours to attain eternal knowledge. The reply was very simple:

"By love may be gotten and holden, by thought never. He comes to us by the cloud of unknowing. The gloves you used separated you from unitive knowledge, for they symbolised personal desire and spiritual craving. Indeed, you acquired much knowledge, but it availed you nothing, as it was learnt second-hand and not attained by experience."

And so the poor man was born again, this time in a frail body with a humble child-like mind. His only sheath was his naked skin. He had no esoteric knowledge to console him. Indeed, his soul remembered just enough of the past to recoil, quite involuntarily, from any contact with occult teaching. He spent his life in the humiliation of suffering, and sacrificed himself for those in need. Faith alone sustained him in his precarious living, until a certain day, not long before he died, when God revealed Himself in the eternal brightness of His effulgent splendour.

He transmitted that splendour to all around him.

8

The End of the Way

IN THIS LIFE we have no abiding city. Everything we achieve on a worldly level seems to be consummated in futility. Our careers founder on the rocks of retirement and decrepitude, the work of our hands falls into disrepair, the nexus of relationships we have so painstakingly built up is demolished by the inroads of time and death, and our money has to be bequeathed to those who often care little for us or about our memory. To me the contemplation of the transience of all mortal things, the vanity of vanities that the Speaker in the Book of Ecclesiastes so fiercely laments, is a source of great joy. How terrible it would be both for us and for those who succeeded us, if we all continued as we are indefinitely.

Nor is there any final spiritual achievement in this life. The most saintly people are more clearly aware of their defects than are their unawakened brethren. There is a time for everything we have achieved and attained in this life to be given over unequivocally to God and to our brothers without any assurance that we will survive the loss. This is the inner meaning of death. It is still the great unknown, the fathomless depth, the impenetrable darkness for all who are yet alive. Even the convinced Spiritualist will find his faith severely taxed at the moment of truth. Intellectual belief (and disbelief) goes before the existential reality of death with its possible sequel of total annihilation. If anyone has reason to accept the after-life it is I, who have been given so many personal proofs — and without recourse to mediums, whose testimony, as I have previously said, is uncertain even at its best. And yet I do not doubt that were I confronted with a sentence of imminent death due to some incurable disease, I would be, at least momentarily, stunned and bereft. I also hope that, when I had adapted myself to the new situation, I would be infused with faith from on high, and carry out my final duties in joy and peace. Yet if this is to be, it will come from God and not my own knowledge about the after-life.

Jesus said, "The hour is come, that the Son of man should be glorified. Verily, verily, I say unto you, except a corn of wheat fall into the ground and die, it abideth alone: but if it die, it bringeth forth much fruit" (John 12:23-24). Jesus, of all men, should have faced His coming trial with joy and exaltation, but throughout the whole Gospel narrative the darkness of His end clouds His ministry. "I have come to bring fire to the earth, and how I wish it were blazing already. There is a baptism I must still receive, and how great is my distress till it is over" (Luke 12:49-50). Immediately after the glorious Transfiguration, He tells His disciples to say nothing of it until after His resurrection. He knew vaguely yet decisively what was in store for Him, that suffering is the essential precursor of glorification. And yet at the commencement of His passsion in the Garden of Gethsemane He was overcome by horror and dismay. "My heart is ready to break with grief; stop here and stay awake" and then the terrible prayer, "Abba, Father, all things are possible to thee; take this cup away from me. Yet not what I will but what thou wilt" (Mark 14:32-36). As He went further into the despair of the whole world, which He voluntarily took upon Himself, so He entered more perfectly than at any time of His ministry His fully human dimension. When He was crucified he called out, "My God, my God, why hast thou forsaken me?" (Mark 15:34, after Psalm 22:1). Yet the final words traditionally ascribed to Him are, "Father, into thy hands I commit my spirit" (Luke 23:46, after Psalm 31:5). There was no intellectual assurance here, only humble hope, the same hope that had sustained the company of Jewish martyrs before Him and after Him.

All this disturbs the esotericist mightily. How could such a great "Master" as Jesus have suffered all these torments?

Surely He knew of occult techniques to master physical and mental pain? Surely He knew the vital role He was playing in the spiritual evolution of humanity? He should have been exultant not bowed down with grief and suffering. But Jesus did not come to show God's might; He came to demonstrate and give God's love. Instead of passing away in a flourish of celestial triumph to His Father in heaven, He took on the full burden of unredeemed humanity, stinking, corrupt, and blind. Each of us has his own burden to bear, and this is enough. But Jesus was encumbered of the psychic darkness of the whole human race, and through its sinfulness, of the whole created world that was put under the dominion of man. His life was consummated in failure. His miraculous powers were unable to stave off the abysmal humiliation that comes of a thwarted mission. There was nothing in any man's personal tragedy that He did not know and bear.

But His life did not end there. He went down into hell to revive the spirits of the inhabitants of the dark regions beyond death. And on the third day He arose decisively from the dead to show Himself once more to the living. Such a resurrection the world has never seen again. It was a resurrection of such magnitude that only one fully divine in nature could accomplish it by the grace of God the Father. "On the human level he was born of David's stock, but on the level of the spirit — the Holy Spirit — he was declared Son of God by a mighty act in that he rose from the dead" (Romans 1:4). "In the days of his earthly life he offered up prayers and petitions, with loud cries and tears, to God who was able to deliver him from the grave. Because of his humble submission his prayer was heard: son though he was, he learned obedience in the school of suffering, and, once perfected, became the source of eternal salvation for all who obey him, named by God high priest in the succession of Melchizedek" (Hebrews 5:8-10).

This is the way of man become perfect. It is a thought to challenge us that Jesus Himself grew in stature and became more perfect in manhood as He approached the end of His ministry and earthly life. The stroke of perfection was the experience of occlusion of the divine knowledge that came with the period of His passion.

To see with fine eyes is natural; to see when one is blinded is supernatural. We in our imperfect lives cannot aspire to such a death and resurrection. But the love of God, shown incontrovertibly in the passion of Christ, assures us that nothing created by Him will ever be allowed to perish. It may, however, take long ages for a wilfully perverse creature to attain salvation.

The Only Way

For a number of years I had known with that indefinable authority that comes from within that I would have to give myself fully to the Church as a priest. I tried, like Jonah, to escape from the implications of this vocation by turning my back on it and pursuing my medical work with greater assiduity. But it was to no avail. My tortuous career was symbolic of the strange journey I was making: a Jew by birth yet directly acquainted with Christ from earliest childhood; brought up in a worldly home yet deeply committed to the mystical path; nurtured by my environment on a mixed diet of rationalism and psychism yet yearning for the life-giving food of the full Catholic faith — which in its finest moments can assimilate all that is true from non-Christian sources, whether scientific, occult, or Eastern; desirous of self-effacing anonymity yet brought increasingly into the public eye by virtue of the inspirational gifts bestowed on me by the Holy Spirit.

I knew that this great contradiction between personality, motivation, and destiny could be resolved only by giving myself fully to God's service. And in the end I submitted my name for consideration as a candidate for ordination. The subsequent stages proceeded with unwonted ease, unlike my secular endeavours, which were never easy and usually frustrated or delayed. The diocesan bishop was the soul of kindness and consideration to me. He waived the usual requirement of a statutory period of training in a theological college in view of my seniority and the considerable amount of time I had devoted to fostering the spiritual life of the Church. In fact, had I been obliged to spend time in a training college, I would perforce have had to relinquish my professional work, at least temporarily. This was above all to be avoided, for the bishop was most emphatic about my continuing the normal course of my medical career even after ordination. Therefore, instead of organised study, I was given the privilege of weekly discussions on theological and pastoral matters with a saintly priest, who was a personal friend. In due course the time drew near for the retreat preliminary to my ordination into the diaconate of the Church of England.

This retreat was to be the most harrowing one I had ever known. It was silent and solitary. There was no conductor — other than the Holy Spirit — and it took place in the middle of winter. I was by this time an experienced retreat conductor, and had led scores of retreatants into the telling silence of truth on a considerable number of occasions. Nor was I a stranger to silence: my early life was fertilised in it, and it was my constant companion during much of my childhood and adolescence. During the dark years of my early adult life, when I was groping blindly for meaning and purpose, it surrounded me like a black pall. It sometimes conjured up fantasies of persecution and emotions of anger and hatred, the great hazards confronting all those who spend too much time alone.

But of the silences I had had in my life, that of this three days' retreat was the darkest in all my experience. In its all-pervasive gloom no secrets were hidden from my spiritual sight. The full structure of my inner life was revealed fearlessly and openly, and I stood as naked before the truth as I believe we all do when we die to the physical body. All the fears, resentments, and inadequacies of my past life flooded tumultuously into consciousness. I was once more the shy, inarticulate little boy, the unsure, diffident young man, the mediocre academician trying to impress others with his brilliance. The long-forgiven troubles with my father came up into awareness once more, telling me that healing is a slow, painful, and progressive process. Here was I, now middle-aged and established professionally, moving into a new field where most of my fellow ordinands would be half my age. Once more the terrible awareness of the incongruity between age and status asserted itself. I had again to be humble and go back to school. I had the gravest doubts about my vocation, and could see numerous psychological inadequacies to account for my decision to become a priest.

There was no one to whom I could turn in my suffering, for in the depths of despair we are all very much alone, apart from God Himself. Had I tried to articulate my inner feelings to even my closest friend among the religious who lived in the house, they would have sounded unbearably trivial and selfish, as indeed they were — at least on a rational level. But what was coming through to me was the history of a soul's life of travail — its hopes and frustrations, its fears and consolations, its vulnerability and its strength. Never did the Bible speak to me as clearly as at that time. I read the Book of Jeremiah with great attention; the Holy Spirit had directed me pointedly to the words and life of that great prophet, the very seal of integrity and as pertinent today as he was long ages ago. I also saw how vastly superior in inspiration Holy Scripture was to even the finest later books on spirituality and prayer. The Bible is indeed the word of the living God, albeit interpreted by the lives and times of the men whom He inspired. And its inspiration comes to us likewise through our own lives irrespective of the theological arguments that have centred on its words.

And so the darkness gathered, until it was impenetrable on the night before ordination. Then sleep overtook me, and I awoke on the Sunday as if born again, young, immature, and innocent. When the time came for me to enter the procession into the church where I was to be ordained, I was aware of a new personality being born in me: calm, possessed, and assured. The words of Revelation rang in my ears as the procession moved towards the altar. "Then I saw a new heaven and a new earth, for the first heaven and the first earth had vanished, and there was no longer any sea. I saw the holy city, Jerusalem, coming down out of heaven from God, made ready like a bride adorned for her husband. I heard a loud voice proclaiming from the throne: 'Now at last God has his dwelling among men! He will dwell among them and they shall be his people, and God himself will be with them. He will wipe every tear from their eyes; and there shall be an end of death, and to mourning and crying and pain; for the old order has passed away' " (Revelation 21:1-4).

Epilogue

And so I was led into the Church's ministry.

My period in the diaconate has been rewarding and illuminating as I serve my necessary apprenticeship prior to the final ordination to the priesthood that awaits me, as I write, in about three months' time. I have found no reason to doubt the rightness of my decision to become a minister of the Church. Although more work has consequently fallen on my shoulders, I find the presence of the Lord a constant support in all my undertakings. Nor has my professional life suffered; indeed, it goes on from strength to strength.

May all this continue as God wills it.

What my future work is to be, I do not know. In myself I find the greatest affinity with the spirit and writings of the mature William Law — not so much the younger man whose *A Serious Call to a Devout and Holy Life* so influenced John Wesley, as the older man made wise by his study of the mystical writings of Jakob Boehme fertilised by his own experience of life. The fruits of this were his two beautiful autumnal works, *The Spirit of Prayer* and *The Spirit of Love*. In them he shows a union of the sacramental devotion of the Catholic Church with the authority of the inner light of man, that great spiritual truth established by the Quaker witness to Christ. Perhaps I too may blaze this trail of a truly Christian universalism, which sees the power of Christ as an inherent property of the human soul (which, as Tertullian pointed out, is naturally Christian) manifesting in the "heathen" saints as well as the Christian ones.

Since William Law's day the glory of the Hindu and Buddhist way to reality has been brought to the notice of the Christian world, and great Catholics, of whom Thomas Merton is the finest contemporary example, have been able to include this wisdom in a fuller understanding of the Catholic faith. I pray to God that all I have learnt in my scientific studies, my psychical experiences and researches, and my mystical illumination may be bequeathed to mankind, so that it may follow the path I have trodden, am treading, and will be treading. It truly involves precarious living, but it does lead "from the unreal to the real, from darkness to light, from death to immortality."